SCARS OF LIGHT

SCARS OF LIGHT

beth goobie

NeWest

Edmonton

First Edition
Second Printing 1998

Canadian Cataloguing in Publication Data
Goobie, Beth, 1959–
  Scars of light

  ISBN 0-920897-73-8

  1. Incest—Poetry. I. Title.
PS8563.08326S32 1994   C811'.54   C94-910499-X
PR9199.3.G663 1994

Credits
Editor for the Press: Rudy Wiebe
Cover and interior design: Diane Jensen
Financial Assistance: NeWest Press and the author gratefully acknowledge the financial assistance of The Canada Council; The Alberta Foundation for the Arts, a beneficiary of the Lottery Fund of the Government of Alberta; and The NeWest Institute for Western Canadian Studies.

Printed and Bound in Canada

NeWest Publishers Limited
Suite 201, 8540-109 Street
Edmonton, Alberta T6G 1E6

Poems in this collection have previously appeared in: *Alberta Anthology; blue buffalo; The Capilano Review; Contemporary Verse 2; The Edmonton Journal; Event; The Fiddlehead; Grain; The Malahat Review; Other Voices; Prism international; Room of One's Own; SansCrit;* and *Tarnation.*

for mark: he was
not the sun or moon,
just a boy
who did not have enough
for what was required

TABLE OF CONTENTS

creed	1
blueprint of face	4
going back	5
what they could tell me	7
around our house	10
basements	12
the garden	14
playground flight	16
in the beginning	18
what lived in the maples	20
from nowhere	21
making the light, the dark and the blue	23
father's world	25
big buck bargains	26
the bank	28
the old library	30
after school	33
within father	36
night travel	37
knowledge	39
black bethlehem star	41
after the resurrection	43
let the children go	45
camping	47
baptism	49
trust	51
the star girl	54

memory code   57

happysad   59

separate rooms   62

bedroom window   64

secret friends   65

two brothers   68

clues   71

altar   74

young men   78

sisters   80

war   82

living with truth   84

the fantasy of no   87

diets   89

high school   91

the look at the fridge   93

just after i knew   97

my brother's wings   98

cleaning out the locker   99

now   101

permission   104

the girl dreams   106

love   108

in the still   109

eight, before definition   111

The author would like to thank the following people
for their support: Pam, Vince, Nora, Carolyn, Lynda, Ken, Norm,
Ruth, The Alberta Foundation for the Arts, all the people
at NeWest Press, especially Rudy Wiebe.

creed

i am going back to find the body.
where was it i left it —
robed and scarlet in a church window,
in the neighbour's pear tree, juice from torn skins
running sweet down the back of the throat?
is the body tied to the old chestnut tree
with the long pink skipping rope, kindergarten boys
circling? did i leave it standing with its brothers
in the evening bedroom, holding the slide
of the naked woman to the window light?
is it in the slide?

so many years, a chalkboard erased.
maybe the body is sewn into the lining
of the stuffed mouse on the childhood bed,
carved into a marble bookend, a piano top bust,
written into diaries, words stretched membrane-thin
over happiness, terror, which it was i could not then
distinguish. those pale limbs, do they lie twisted,
gently glowing under the clawed feet of the bath tub,
radiator, coffee table? can some part of the dark
paneled floorboards, doorframes, an uneven stair
be lifted and there it will be, folded up,
a smile worked onto its face? maybe
in those holocaust walls. most of the house walls
were off-white, made up of warped and naked bodies,
heads turned away, arms stretched up to keep the ceiling,
the overhead light, the cosmos in place. i thought
these were the bodies of those who had suffered
in the past, saints of the early church,
victims of wars. now i see they are all me,
one girl body self-divided into bodies, each a fraction,
self-separated, self-protected against the whole of one
experience, though they always stood shoulder to shoulder
within the same breath, heartbeat, cemented
together keeping out the wind.

i remember granite bones in the citroen's back seat,
father at the wheel. i remember the sandbag heart
in a series of desks, watching classmates
send themselves across the room like invisible
hawks and pigeons. adolescent mornings
one of the bodies would come awake, finger
the thick cream on the underwear crotch,
left behind by the night bodies. the morning body
was confused; this belonged to someone else,
another time, place. but whose? she did not know
the others, did not know she rose from anything
but the moan and shift of flesh-coloured dreams.

in the suicidal years, the body is its own tombstone.
i lived above the neck. it was the only way
to survive. now i am going back down into the bowels.
there will be no mercy. i will dig into father's
balls to find the seed. i will lift the foetus out
of my mother's gut, stellar in its skin, carry it
to safety. i will find the body in corner dust balls,
the cremated ashes of my brother's death.
i will find it if i have to become
gravedigger, sleepwalking nightwatcher, leech,
the stone in your throat you must learn to speak
around. to find the body, i will become killer
of family, friend, god.

in old testament time, a single woman could
lay herself at the foot of a man's bed,
give him the choice to take her into his harem
or have her killed.
when ruth placed her body in boaz's tent,
she did not wait to discover tolerance or murder lust;
she floated up and away, left flesh
behind like a broken promise,
a wine bottle that had not properly sealed,
kept the spirit in, what mattered out.

i have seen her in a dream, a vague pink glow.
she is headed back. she will bring that body
out with her, alive.

in the distance, boaz sees her coming,
begins to dig his own grave.

blueprint of face

when the brother dies, he steps out of his photographs.
his face wants off the bone. the rest of ours follow.
someone has gone and cut all our faces out of my memory.
in my head, they arrange in a circle around
that point in time, the informing of the suicide.
inside, this tunnel of time keeps turning
the circle all funny. faces blur, overlap.
parts of them get lost, show up on someone else's
skull. father stares out of my brother's eyes.
maybe that always was.

we bury a face with the body. it is not that of the dead.
in the church pew row, we peel off our own,
drop them into the offering plate, all we have left
to give god. from the coffin, in turn,
each of us scoops one handful of face
from the dead brain. i choose the feature
from which i am to build my new face,
select the shred of his expression that haunts me
most, lives in my peripheral vision.
the mouth? the nose? the eye.

i see from photographs
that our faces are coming along, though none is yet
complete. my mother builds little onto the patch of face
she chose. is this loyalty? father, hidden behind a rembrandt
beard, is difficult to assess; some of his forehead is gone.
in conversations, we talk around the name, blueprint
of the unspoken, try to remember, always before words
the name is *mark,* so that it will not be spoken
as alive, out of context. my mother used to scramble
our five names, call them all when she wanted one.
this habit is dangerous, with death we are precise,
step carefully about structures of overlapping face, though
we are face within face within face always becoming
one another.

going back

my hometown unrolls before me like a pop-up map.
from our house, the ottawa street hill dives
in summer raw green, autumn umber, november
and its black sobbing trees, toward the high school,
exhibition park, the water tower. you can follow
the two concrete miles of sidewalk cracks
we walked to the christian school where playground
galaxies of children still swirl over gravel,
but redbrick memories of the old ymca,
the public library have been torn down.
the eaton's centre has wiped out the greyhound
bus terminal. sears and the odeon have migrated
to the malls. even the laura secord shop,
it secrets wrapped in chocolate musk,
the smiling grey-haired ladies, gone now,
though the banks are in place, and the churches —
anglican, presbyterian, united — locked
into this earth, their spires, greystone prayer,
the weather-vane cock sent up daily
over bookstores, cafes along quebec street.

on the hill above everything, church of our lady's
stained glass windows blossom in its sides
like flowers on time lapse film. you climb
from street level up the hillside steps,
traffic and the city going faint below. your heart
beats its wings to take you to these heights,
on the top step the church still soars above you,
pulls your spirit out through your pores
up along the stone walls to black spire tips,
anchors in a fast-moving sky. then in through
heavy front doors, opening like a bible.
walls echo your breathing. you are in
the circle of forever each church is,
have stepped into a paperweight, repentance

briefly turning your world upside down,
then again upright; divinity descends slow,
touches your skin.

in exhibition park, the maples still there,
whispering the same warnings i do not understand.
leaves flee trees as if before an invasion.
swings rock, empty. children and dogs have gone home.
i sit alone in the baseball stands, watch the wind
kick up dust at home plate, then come at me
with giant wings. i am lifted above streets
that rein the trees into thin lines, swoop
in a casual arc of flight that takes in
the mock victorian suburbs, stone road mall,
the university agricultural farms.

approaching home, the wind drops me at the foot
of the hill. it rises, cast in late afternoon amber
like mount sinai toward the house on ottawa street.
when i was six, this city block ran down toward me
like the end of the world and finally there was
the driveway to the brownred side door carved
with the dangerous flowers.

i think inside is my mother, surrounded by the smells
of cheese or roast beef. she has completed her daily
devotional, today's bible chapter, prayed that each of us
will walk within the invisible fist of god.
from the living-room, music from father's studio,
fingers of bartók and brahms, a stronger grasp.

this place will not open, the house gone quiet,
window-shades heavy-lidded, doors healed shut.
it is now the only dark place in this city
torched by spring, colours violent,
gouging out the earth.

what they could tell me

pressed against the brick of the public high school,
i swim around the walls again and again.
it is now and to those inside i am the ghost
of the future. when i grab the door handle,
my hand, empty of flesh, passes through it.
around the cycle of these walls, i drag myself.
trying to press through to the past, i have rubbed
my skin down to the blood. i want to see the face
of my old history teacher, close up, pulled out
of its blur. he used to point toy cannons at us,
raise his index finger above his head, close his eyes,
then drop it down upon the seating plan like a bomb.
you could explode when called upon. he was a vet.
for him it was a game and he was a good man
as was my french teacher, lean, stretched out
like a pulled elastic, body connected by surrealistic
joints. later, he found religion. then, it was chess.

my english teacher found cancer but survived.
she looked at me once as if she saw the death cells
in me. it was after my brother's suicide.
in a class assignment, i had called myself an animal
for hating him. her dark eyes looked at me;
they began a journey into me. *i'm concerned about you,*
she said. she was taking me with her
into myself. i had to turn away. *i'm fine,*
i told her. within seconds, i had folded the moment
into a memory i would hand back to myself, time
after time, smoothed with handling, seamless with regret.

among the thousand kids in the cafeteria, it was easier.
i settled with the girls from the 4H club
who rode the orange buses, slid their lunches
out of brown bags and wax paper
while kids from the city formed long lines

7

for french fries and gravy on pressed cardboard plates.
there was the friend whose fireman father died in the flames,
the other who lived with her mother waiting
against the return of an alcoholic father
found finally neckbroken at the bottom of stairs.
i watched them then, like a caped man,
arm drawn up over the face so only the eyes showed,
and i calculated the angle of freedom in their shoulders,
assessed the way their eyes drifted in and out
of their own gaze.

the fireman's daughter continued on in a joy
that had always lived in her as if it belonged there,
belonged like breathing. laughter swept through her
the way wind picks up an entire horizon.
the other girl, she had a smile that flickered
through the sands of her face and the waves,
they kept rushing over and over.
i want to touch all their faces, these girls—
feel the temperatures of their skins, their heartbeats
swimming fluid as fish under my fingertips, pulsing
through to me now. i want to ask,

have you seen a girl named beth,
the one with the railroad tracks across her smile,
the one who sits near the doorway whenever possible,
floats above her own body like a parachute
over enemy territory? have you seen the fear rise
in her, wall of fire within wall of skin,
burning out her throat and brain,
the ashes that meander from her mouth?
watch, if you can, for the heart in her
desperate to spawn and die
not into another but into herself.
tell her, for me, the birthing grounds are where
they have always been. they will wait for her
forever and she will come home,

but these girls turn their faces, stricken with youth,
beauty, the power pulled out of them like fingernails,
turn toward the adult i have become
hovering indistinct before them, dust in the light.
we have seen beth, they say.
she had a bologna sandwich, made words, here and there.
she is a busy girl, always somewhere to move on to.
she was here a minute ago. you could have told her
yourself, but as you can see you have missed her
and now she is gone.

around our house

the red brick house on ottawa street.
three storeys high, it rose out of the earth,
dark-windowed, reflecting the street back onto itself.
shingle-quilted snow on its peaked roof
drifted into wintergrey sky. autumns,
squirrels scrabbled in the eaves troughs,
balanced chestnuts, glossbrown diaries between paws.
summers, invisible cicadas tore our ears wide open.
spring, the forsythia bush exploded into yellow
and the geraniums, fists of colour,
guarded the veranda.

the trees on our block were taller than the houses,
full of wings, but kept for this earth.
across the street, behind the green and white clapboard,
willows wove in and out of sky, fingered
the late afternoon sun. our front lawn maple
spread above the rooftop like a promise whispered
to that self curled into the inner ear and slow-
moving always with sleep; it filled windows
on each floor, a rustling green heavy in our nostrils
with the coming of rain.

out back, a small rectangle of tire-rutted grass.
the chain link fence, slanted at a crazy angle,
rammed by cars that grumbled along the alley.
back there, my mother grew rhubarb and tomatoes
in a thin line along the fence, uncurled the garden
hose from its lime green circles hooked
over the handle on the house wall.

years back, a hazy swing set, a laundry tree,
the red and white striped home-sewn bedsheets
belled out, snapping in the wind and rushes
of soap scent, the rattle of wooden clothespins

in tin containers. the fence loomed higher than my hands
could reach. sky above my head ran on without
wire mesh through its winds, dreams
softly volatile, changes in direction.

basements

at the back door landing, the ice box in the wall
filled with blue mittens, long white scarves,
balaclavas, toques. to the left, the basement
stairwell, painted grey descent, hollowed out
by decades coming and going. inside, the stone wall
is pocked, damp to the touch, the shelf lined
with varnish tins, wrenches, bicycle pumps.
as your knees bend to take you down each step,
the smell of must and apples rises.
you are underground. on the basement floor,
small metal drain lids, grimy medusa faces
cover the tunnels that run straight down
into the earth's gut. you have heard
of the possibilities that can crawl up out of them,
listen to the warnings when your foot grinds
the lids against the cold stone floor.

the furnace room, its shelves of preserves.
jars of peach-fleshed hearts and summer guts.
for dessert, we devour dreams of our selves.
back in a corner, the missionary trunks my mother
took to germany on her 50s baptist crusade.
closer to the door, this week's garbage,
the huge grey furnace, grumbling and warm.
above this room, father's music studio.
chopin, brahms, saturate the floorboards,
soak through in muffled, coagulated sound.
across the ceiling above you he shifts,
the dark creaking that bears his weight.

at the basement's far end, the soundproofed practise studio.
click of the fluorescent lamp and you appear
in a cone of light at the old upright piano,
set the *toronto conservatory* book on the ledge,
flattened along its binding. before your hands

float out across the black and cracked beige keys,
sound is growing in your bones.
it begins as the thin line of your vertebrae,
swells out across your heart like a rib-cage,
crests into the magnificent curves that support
and contain your groin. you become liszt's message
of light and being. it comes to you
sure as a cavalry regiment, flowing through oceans,
rivers, groundwater, up the long dark drain tunnels;
medusa's whisper enters this small circle of light.
note to note, you make your way,
small stars come to life on your fingertips,
you are draped in nebulae and more dark
beyond you, leads you
further in.

the garden

there were two ways into our house. at each door
the dark wood paneling began. the grain of it
swam and slid in circles smooth to the touch,
scalloped and curved like fairy tales
but it sank deeper than the skin
along the finger that traced its belled edge.
this treeline along floorboards, around doorways,
closets, windows, this dark grain of wood
pulled you far under the surface gleam, down
into a murky history, the night life of trees.
there under the kitchen's white paint, beneath
the varnish and stain of the rest of the house,
the wood linked every room, every entrance
to the beyond within a common horizon.

in the front lobby, the thin bodies of trees
rose stark in oak pillars, lilies dug into each side.
this was the darkest place in the house, entry
to father's studio where primrose patterned
lace slanted the outside light and
frosted hollyhocks on overhead lamps threw
shadow flowers over the wall-sized bookcase,
into the eyes of beethoven frowning
from the green marble mantel.
one studio wall became two sliding doors,
again the mellow brown of wood carved to flowers
that opened onto the dull light of the dining-room
corner lamps. roses twisted along the coffee table edge,
baby's breath withered in the oriental vase,
daffodils drifted down walls and
daisies crocheted into off-white meadows
sprawled across the back of the couch.
next to the cuckoo clock hung the oil painting
of a pristine mountain and lake
my parents received on their wedding day.

in this place, silence pressed down, over and across
a mouth that slurred the muscles of my face,
terrible and weighted with the one imploded scream.
arms hung, strange with heaviness. i could not tell
what held me down, what sadness bred in me
fell soft, quiet as snow through my chest,
but i heard the voices, slight and whispery,
that sifted out of the leather-bound hassock,
the dining table eagle claws, the studio piano,
music waiting in its gut.

these flowers torn from their roots that fill this house,
the voices said, *the african violets stamped*
into the kitchen tabletop, the huge carnation you pick out of
your bedspread, the ferns that riot across your headboard
and the bones of trees moaning leaves stripped too early—
this is a false garden. listen to your own mouth,
sealed against the inner voice that beckons, pleads,
whimpers your own name. it calls from your gut,
that place between collarbone and high thighs
where you do not let yourself exist. the voice calls
and calls and your throat, it has lengthened
into a long dark stem, long as the years that go back
to the time your lips were plucked from your face
like a delicate veined blossom,
then placed on the tea cup, the curtain,
the deadly quiet wall.

playground flight

the way the world spun round.
you sit on the wooden circle bench,
hands tight around the metal grip,
your heart crouched in your throat, ready
to leap. your mother is beside you,
leans into her knees and elbows, begins to push
into the circle. grins of brothers, sisters,
sky, trees, swing, concession booth
slide into one another as mother
works up speed, gasps and steps back, drops
away into a background whirling grass, sky,
like an impressionist's painting. all trees become
one tree, extended. the concession booth
flicks at the brain, here and gone, here and gone.
great invisible hands push out from the circle's center
up your chest, around your throat.
you lean back.

slowly, the giant sleeping wings in your head unfold.
you stretch out, lean further back.
the sky, between the blurred circle of tree, tilts
toward you like a plate, takes over your eyes
and the wings in your brain reach up and out,
a huge pulse of up and out
as the circles sliding in your skull widen
and the blue space of sky swallows, takes you in.

the world slows. the sky withdraws to its place
above the trees. unmoving, the booth sits
on the other side of the park. still, you hang,
head back from your neck. your heels
return to earth, dragged along in the dirt,
another small ridge, grounded circle.
your mother helps you off the bench. as you stand,
the wings, a slight protest in your brain,

keep you off balance, in dreams
that settle, return to rest. blinking,
you find your feet again in shoes, linear momentum,
the walk toward home.

in the beginning

trees over the exhibition park wading pool
lean in, warm dark breath that wafts
through quick sparks of sun. you sit
on the cement edge of the smell of chlorine;
splashes and shrieks lap halfway to your knees.
deep heat nibbles at your scalp, swirls sluggish
in shoulders, contentment a shadow
slow falling through your bones.
on your stomach, your swimsuit clings, cool, wet,
and between your legs; you lower yourself
again into the water's warm mouth.
at the surface skipping light, the swimsuit skirt
lifts, protests a moment and is pulled under.
now the water is everywhere.
it nudges and licks like summer nights when father
is gone to study at the american university
and your mother's voice rising up out of white pages
pools like lamplight, the circle-throbbing cricket song,
the wash inside the conch shell that continues
long in your ear after day pulls away

and you sleep. the water is like dreaming.
you float on this afternoon. each part of you
lifts up out of its own heaviness.
bones slide away from each other,
muscles untwine and water strokes,
slips into each pore, into the lips between
your legs until you are all water,
inside you are quiet whispering water,
your face ripples away like light, you are
about to be washed out to sea.

called into the shade
under the maples and evergreens,
you jump between wet feet as your mother

rubs out your shivers with thin striped towels.
now your face, arms, legs are yours again,
solid and rough with heat but still the water
shifts and sighs under the wet suit
where nipples glow like beach-wet pebbles
and the lower lips curl into themselves.
you pull fir needles from between your toes,
slide half-wet feet into canvas runners
and in your ears you are still part
of the moon-rippled lakes that murmur
endless in the belly of the earth,
the deepest parts of night.

then your fingers tug sticky paper
from the three-coloured popsicles,
blue, white, pink sold at the concession booth.
sweetness melts cold into your mouth,
there is the smell of wet wood sticks.
throwing them away, you crook elbows
around chains that weave down out of the sun.
the swing seat presses hard against bum bones,
warm and pulling secrets just a little apart.
behind you the scent, the slight moan
of your mother comes and goes.
knees bent, shoelaces dangling, horizon
rising and falling, you are again motion,
you could let go, you could be sky.

what lived in the maples

summer deep in the lung, evening in the mouth,
swallows above the paisley street bus stop.
i rode the rustling trees, summer-long,
my body composed of their sound, veined
in maples, their dark green whisper,
smudges of sleep. the trees were old explorer
ships at full sail. they were houses, leaves instead
of bricks, let in wind, a legion of night moths
hovering about porch and streetlight and as long
as the maples shushed, moaned and hummed,
i moved within myself, held together
as a house of leaves

          i would turn into night, into
the exquisite terror of dreams and the rustling
would mount, a high wind in my blood,
me blown to torn-off leaves, moths
on one wing sent wheeling inward to that
unbreathing cosmos hunched in my gut.
i could go anywhere but there.
it was the half-winged moths, flickers of white,
i let go like a message, a sob sent into that black
from the ark

          life in their mouths,
they never came back.

from nowhere

after the plane traced itself soundless across
the cool blue and was gone, those hard smoke
trails could have come from nowhere.
far below, down among city streets,
heat ate up sidewalks and verandas,
banisters so white, they argued with the eye.
tight braids rooted to my scalp, bite of metal
rollerskate grips against canvas runners,
i circled my block, paisley jumpsuit rubbing
a shoulder-burn raw. through the double thunk
of summer sidewalks, i coasted queasy afternoons
toward my mother's back door call.
my brothers rode the bright air in on their bikes,
my sisters ran, sinking into soft flip flop soles,
plastic flowers enormous across their toes.

anxiety scratched mosquito bites on our legs.
koolaid popsicles gave their slow suck
as my mother's wrist worked them out
of their moulds. sometimes she watched us,
our lips stretched to worry the cold sweet
with tongues. she sat on the hot back step,
tight and tense as a railway yard, heart beating
against the distance whispering in its tracks,
you could go so far, you could go

away from this. above in the far-away, i could see
silent things happen, white smoke losing outlines
the way the unspoken drifts into sighs,
vague as dreams, over just-open lips.
we licked purple popsicle drops from our arms as
faces from our street gave greetings, got in and out
of car door slams. solid and bright-edged,
all this could ripple in the day heat, the membrane
of light give way and sudden night lean in,

forearm across my throat, giving me its mouth again,
while the man-voice that spoke only in my head
said, *now this is the way you french kiss.*

beside me, sisters wiped their purple-stained
grins. in our home, dimensions came and went;
father was never there until he walked his body,
hard and real, into the room and then
he had always been walking in and you
had always been waiting—if you don't know
when something's coming, it's always coming.
secrets twisted into us like corkscrews. unvoiced,
they kept the front veranda geraniums in bloom,
swung each screen door back into its frame,
brought the call of our mother out of the same
face and mouth. miles above us,
passengers of the sky faded to nothing.
they had never been there.

making the light, the dark and the blue

my mother made candles from crayons she collected
leftover from our sunshine, our happy faces, our green-
peaked roofs. there were yoghurt containers of red and blue
stubs she kept on the pantry shelf behind the brown curtain,
then melted in pots on the stove. chunks of ice held
the long line of wick upright as the hot wax poured
from my mother's hand into milk cartons, sizzled
across the creak and fissure of ice.

when my mother finished high school, she moved far away
from the family farm to illinois, germany, georgia, canada
but the candles she made for us were the blue of montana
sky, the blue of heaven created by light coming
from such a distance, the blue of her guarded gaze,
blue as the raised veins that ran bodyside her wrists.
my mother said her father doted on the daughter
born in america, sat by her evenings as constellations
of a different sky fell out of her mouth. at six,
she learned to read english, play the piano.
forty years of ukraine deepened behind him in corner
shadows. my mother became a high school thespian, joined
the debating team. her bone-thin mother removed herself
daily to the small hill behind the house, outlined against
all that blue and the montana wind in fierce prayer.
in the 40s, my mother and her mother worked
on the ships that took the men to sea and war, washed down
the decks, brought back the money of women to the farm
and when her father sent his daughter to college,
he saw her rise like the stars and stripes to where she
flew against the sun in a heart-burst of trumpet and drum.

but with all that love, my mother never went back except
surrounded by us one summer i was four and their deaths
the year i was eleven. after this, she spoke of her mother's
survival through the ten years her father left his wife

and children in ukraine, went to america to prepare
a place for them. while they waited, my grandmother
waded through swamps with one daughter and sons, bullets
tearing fear wide open above their heads. the girl's lungs
filled with blue and she died. ten years later the husband
came back, sought until he found them, bought clothes, a way
out. she had to re-learn him, he had to re-learn her.
the first and only time he raised his body against hers,
she took that bruise to the polson montana police station
and charged him in five per cent english. he paid his fine,
sobbed an apology in front of the german baptist congregation
and their american daughter was born. *we were happy,*
we yelled and screamed politics in the kitchen
until it bounced and rolled off the walls,
my mother said. *i wish i had gone back*

more often. as i watched, she tore the milk carton back
from the hardened blue body formed around the now-melted
ice, lit the wick, turned off the overhead light.
the white kitchen softened, the ceiling far above us
disappeared, montana and ukraine uneasy, shifted dark
about us. then the walls came in, huddled around
the flame that danced in and out of the glowing places
melted into the night-blue wax, stars gouged out,
my mother's face over the fire flickering in and out
of shadow, exquisite in the patterns
of its truths.

father's world

father is in that space on the other side of sound.
brahms, weighted with beard, crowds his shoulders
and voices of heavier angels, foreheads lined
with symphonies, introspective fugues,
whisper down the conch shell passage of his ears.
he reads dostoevsky, quotes christ.

the piano keyboard stretches before his hands,
a continent uninhabited by the mundane.
melody, a movement in the air, writhes
in each finger, lifts out to touch
beethoven, gershwin, debussy,
his own inner drift of sound,
the crowd of unworded voices hovering in his ears,
calling him in.

as he spreads church choruses across sunday mornings,
the cosmos shifts, wind-twisted, in his brain.
the far side of the sanctuary recedes.
he sheds these days of earth, faces
of defeat, the ordinary flesh and words,
follows the wind in his hands.
voices leave his mouth as small angels
in one true line.

this moment, he spills out
of fingers and mouth into spirit into glory,
church window stained glass figures
leave their metal outlines.
the congregation, hymnals clutched, rise
out of their throats in an ascending spiral,
evening blue, scarlet, forest green,
colours of their faith.

big buck bargains

the big buck store on yarmouth was a warehouse
of possibility. brown barrels of cutlery, tea towels,
barbie dolls, and men's socks rose, papery
smooth to their metal rims. elbow joint
crooked over the barrel lip, i could trace
the plaid weave of a hundred dish cloths,
not the grey-stained underwear mothers
dipped into the swish and sigh of dying suds.
the second floor was a dusty yawn
of far-off walls and ceiling.
among the shelved dolls, the scent of plastic
smiles and eyes rose through my nose and brain
like yeast. boxed in and staring through cellophane,
arms and legs splayed out, manufactured helplessness,
but the dolls were built hard and tough to take it;
all you needed was the price of admission:
$12.95 in the usa, $10.95 in canada.

adults, their polyester stomachs pushing over
elasticized waistbands, wandered through dust motes
and the ring of downstairs cash registers
where my sister pam stood at a till,
chin and forearm trusting the counter linoleum,
pigtails waving like flags, her brown eyes
two questions that demanded answers.
zipped into a stretched acrylic bosom, a clerk's
smile spread across her green eyelids,
her startled peony cheeks, like a new stroke
in a watercolour painting. as she leaned
into pam's chatter and pointing finger,
explained big buck's bargains and sales,
my brother vince, just off to the left behind
paul newman and robert redford, guns and grins
on the magazine rack, stuffed pockets
he had layered over his thin chest and thighs

with *lifesavers, double bubble,* candy necklaces
you chewed off until only the wet saliva string
rubbed around your multi-coloured throat.
finally vince rustled, heavy-hipped, past pam
and she ducked out of the clerk's attention,
pushed with her brother, bodies brief and dark
in the rectangles of light that were the push-out doors.

down streets that throbbed with sun,
across potholes that sagged with softening tar,
past storefronts rippling in the heat
with the frown of a man searching
his butt pocket for the missing wallet,
my sister and brother ran, mouths and hands
stained bright candy blues and reds,
boxes, price tags and cellophane wrap keeping pace
invisible and all in place around them.

the bank

in the two large pockets of the navy blue apron
with the scarlet ribbing, my mother carried
the family bank. as she peeled carrots,
went up and down stairs, bent into the smells
of the oven, her body rustled and clicked within itself
like her partial when she chewed.
everywhere she went the sounds followed her,
whispering possibilities, the values of capitalism.
only on sundays or weekend company for dinner
did she take the apron off, trust god
with its hiding place, the way i requested
divine protection for my diary but never got it.

my mother thought to teach us each act builds
a palace or prison we are later to inhabit;
she bought hundreds of poker chips
from the nearest variety store—red, white, blue
plastic discs of hope. we earned one white chip
for brushing our teeth, one red chip for making
the bed, two blue for washing dishes.
two white chips equalled one blue or red,
two blue or red chips equalled one nickel,
a half hour of tv or friday night treats—
chocolate chips, peanuts, raisins,
maybe some salt'n vinegar chips.

at first my mother kept the bank
in large peanut butter jars behind
the brown pantry curtain. her eyes searched
beyond our toothpaste breath for rotting food
particles, under beds tucked into daylight
for what we could not bring with us out of sleep.
everything began to add up to the click
of the poker chip. red, white, blue stacks mounted
on my bookshelf like an attitude, an IQ score,

a term report card. in this system of becoming,
we learned the two choices: have or have not.
so my brothers and sisters taught my mother
a lesson in enterprise.
the bank behind the brown curtain began to sink
at unexpected rates, the gambler, the gangster,
the prostitute staring back from her own children's eyes

and my mother began to feel the choices she had built
herself into. bone by bone, breast by breast,
she became the state, the status quo, the pearly gates;
big brother looked out of her gaze, measured
the millimeters of our movements, hands under the table,
behind our backs, carefully fingering our sins.

my mother poured the bank into two plastic bags,
one for each navy blue pocket, secured them
with twist ties and her own warm body,
the way it never rested, tangential as she darted
from one room to the next. now at her approach,
the weight of a hundred small judgements clicked
with each step. after chores, my reward
rose up out of her belly, my hand clutched
at the plastic circle, certainty in my grip.
with each dish dried, bible verse memorized,
each brief line of anger smoothed out of my bedsheets,
i turned from a vague awareness of the second fork
in the road, the way it wandered off
down into the green shadows of my throat,
the wilderness that splayed itself out somewhere there.

system established, there was no forgiveness,
no gift. the only way out was to grow up
but my child's body could not get ahead
of itself, marched me along the straight and narrow
that led back to my mother. she kept me suckling,
infantile, on her esteem. each choice left me
wrecked on her approval like a birth.

the old library

the old public library pulled the wrath of the gods
down onto norfolk street to where it scowled
opposite the ymca. in archaic brick, these two
glowered over traffic that had built up
like a headache over the years. located in a century
and a city blueprint sketched out around
john galt's outstretched hand, the buildings frowned
upon street level like michelangelo jehovahs.
dr. seuss and *curious george* under my arm,
i climbed front stairs that spread out like a beard,
each foot closer to the gloom that lined
the building's forehead. children entered as thieves,
their bodies stole silence from the walls,
the adults positioned under lamps like half-lit thoughts,
chests curved in to muffle the beat of life.
it was like opening an adult book, the mind
of someone who does not want you there.
in the old library, no one disturbed melancholia,
the millennia of its ongoing choice.

when i was seven the two mammoths on norfolk
were torn out of the sky, making way
for apartments and a new library,
both cloud-grey with wheelchair access,
walls of windows, a greater place of light.
this place belonged to the children.
tables, anxious to please, ran around themselves
in circles. orange plastic chairs squatted
close to the floor. rainbow-draped books shouted
out from the shelves, full of powerful children
(maybe not too powerful) who defeated space aliens,
diamond smugglers, neighbourhood bullies,
even the devil perhaps but never god.
saturday mornings, leotards and corduroy
rustled in the *story hour* room.

here a librarian sent her voice out,
the beginnings of wind, while we peered at her,
rows of small fierce eyes, waiting for her thin words
to find our wings. sometimes a guest writer visited.
once, jean little, in her careful body,
reached into the moment and took out the front
of her prosthetic eye. we stared
at the white glowing ball left in the socket.
this belonged in the old library

she had brought it into the new, where
children learn to put words adults give them
to everything. *feeling yes, feeling no* featured
in the video section, keeps streets of strangers,
perhaps the dentist, the uncle, at bay,
but still the shape of father steps out of the wall
of sleep; flights of fantasy are allowed
as long as the body is left behind.
in the old library, books roosted on shelves,
waited for the moment i opened their hearts,
rose up with the white lift of the page
into weightlessness, a morning sky that floated
on and on beyond words, the sigh of the binding
as the covers closed on the last page of day
and the lights turned out. the first books
built places beyond the horizon of this face,
this bone; the first books built sky

the way it was in the old library.
quiet between my lungs, i watched *somewhere* weave itself,
thin blue with streaks of rose and peach
across the dome of closed eyelids, the peak of the brain,
the romanesque arch of my skull.
then i began to rise up out of the sounds
of my own breathing, the muffled day-long echoes
of small night moans, the regular give of bedsprings
there in my chest, groin, my thin white thighs.

i had learned the language of the body—
it was the sound of breath leaving,
and from the mouth, it was silence

but i could rise through the old library air,
shadowy and suspicious, up through
ceilings that dissolved into somewhere else,
for there were galaxies to weave through walls,
skies to fingerpaint over ceilings, the kingdom of
heaven among us now, just as jesus said.

after school

at breakfast, our faces shrank and expanded
in rotating cereal spoons. the day could go either way,
full of moments that picked themselves up like tea cups
and poured us down someone else's throat.
we waited for god to drop the rubber ball,
scoop one of us up in a divine game of jacks.
at the christian elementary school on water street
we were washed in blood, lined up for inspections
of ears, teeth and fingernails, checkmarks posted daily
on classroom hygiene charts. teachers missed
the snakes that hid in toilet bowls, raised up
and entered, the bowels a live place nobody monitored
for cleanliness, but godliness was more important;
we scattered its jagged light the way the boy
with the stutter mangled syllables.
his grade five three-minute speech chewed up eighteen
while the rest of us snickered savage sympathy
and the teacher's eyes rested on the clock.

resolution hung on my brothers, thin as tee shirts. allday,
boys crowded them into bathroom walls, playground fences.
allday teachers watched girls skip double-dutch.
school over, push-handle doors burst into the ribs
of late afternoon maples that stitched sky to ground.
sun sinking down the edinburgh road hill tossed
flames of glass across riverside apartment blocks, homes.
boys pursued by brothers along sidewalks
that cupped the last smudged light, threats adrift
like twilight along the lilac hedges. my brothers
had become their tradition, predictable as morning prayer,
but sometimes god let someone else go down,
arms up so there was no face,
and rage would rise in my brother mark, stark
as a winter tree. he would kick, kickkickkickkick,
the body at his foot giving way like a moan,

he would do this now the way it was always done to him,
roll all their fury into his own thin self,
absolute—this was what life wanted
and no one's motherlove, no one's denial
would get near until fatigue took his muscles back
and there was the face of another, blurred human
in the blue snow, its body the shape
of a man running, the way we woke from dreams,
bedsheets twisted terror around our legs,
screams pitched so high only wolves heard.

sometimes, we pieced ourselves together the way
my brother vince screwed the leg back into the table
after father beat him with it. past the afterschool
apocalypse, the five of us collected.
hot pennies of pain surfaced in my brothers,
we sisters walked footprints of snow around them,
wanting our feet to take us somewhere new, somewhere
kind. once a factory dumped soap waste into the river,
killed the fish but for miles, suds rose thirty feet
off the water, spread a hundred feet up either bank.
that day the pack pounded down the hill toward
the river, my brothers' dark outlines the first to disappear
into a million pink-blue suds, the soft overhead whisper
of hearts breaking all around. paradise—
god touched earth and cradled us. that day,
childhood was caught off guard by wonder.
we passed each other, vague and silent shapes,
spun pirouettes in a thousand sunsets dying
over and over in our outstretched hands.

mostly, miracles hid themselves like guardian angels.
we had to find gifts to give ourselves, so small
no one else would notice. we pulled gum
off home-bound sidewalks to chew, traded bottles
at corner stores for two cent bags of broken candy,
left stones on the edinburgh tracks to derail

passing trains. evening cars went by,
their headlights blurred carnations in the dusk.
at the end of the day was the ottawa street hill,
just before dark. here my sister pam,
the tread worn off her hand-me-down white wellingtons,
hung onto my brother mark's coat. he would press
his full weight into one boot, then another,
and pull her giggles up the icy slope.

within father

father never saw us. the eyes
in his face shone with a reflected light.
always, he looked inward, searching
for its source, moved as if underwater,
in some murky dark.

when father came into a room,
he was larger than his size,
of old testament dimensions. he would
sacrifice his son if an angel spoke
the burning words. he would find
the message. he prowled late at night
downstairs, read thick books about revelation
and communism, opened and closed the fridge.
when we heard the sound of his weight,
immense as night on each stair
coming into our dreams,
we shrank, not knowing
what he carried, what inner landscapes
of rage, that distant light.

we were the unseen, the unheard. we waited
for him to pass through our presence,
leave us, small rowboats tied to a wharf
at the surface of his existence,
rocking in our skins.

night travel

when i turned out the bedroom light, i left
the door open so the hall light lit up amber
crossing the floorboards toward my bed.
from my pillow-view, the doorway slanted
crazy as a van gogh painting. i imagined
the other darkened rooms that led off this hall,
my sisters, brothers, foetal and flannel,
classmates, all the children of the world curled
around that thumb in the mouth and staring
at this in-between place of light;
just before sleep, it joined all of us

and when my mother went to bed, she came around,
closed each door. framed one last moment
in the disappearing hall, her soft *goodnight*
turned the bedroom into a dimension sealed off
from everywhere else, as complete and dark
as the human heart, what was carried there.
only the line of light under the closed door.
it was an anchor keeping me awake, in the here
and now, not the secret world and language
my mother closed me into each night she whispered
bon voyage and sleep began to carve larger versions
of myself around me like a russian doll set.
layer upon layer grew between me and what
was coming; the little me who loved daddy
had so far to go, no rest for the weary,
but i was experienced at night travel,
dug deep into a dark where no star had yet been
born. then somewhere in the hall i left behind,
a door opened. its click threw an inner switch,
my every nerve a sudden brilliant tunnel,
simultaneous fathers walked each one toward
doors that took them farther in, wherever
they wanted. i built so many walls;

there was no wall without a door these fathers
did not seek, no part of my skin that was not
an opening they broke and entered. mother closed;
father opened, for he owned the house and everything
in it—its night and day, its screams, its silence.
layer after layer, he ripped his way through,
whether it was mouth, bum, cunt, it was
count, count, count until it's all over,
the way you count hydro poles along the highway,
seconds on the clock, 4/4 in the school band—
so good at keeping time and no one knows why

especially the part of me that belonged in the day—
world of family portraits, tv sitcoms, children's lit.
blinking and gummy-eyed, this me
yawned its way out of an absolute dark,
back through holes fathers had torn into my flesh,
doorways left open for a quick return through layers
of self i laid down like the canadian shield—
terror, hatred, rage, pain, grief—
through to the only door still closed,
the door of love and forgetting, my mother
opening it to call, *time to get up.* beyond her
the hall now rested dark, and in the rooms
clustered around it, children stretched into
dawn, our first movements, slow, curved
as a question mark.

knowledge

i wanted a life.
that's what it came down to, in the end
and truth stood in the way. eve, she was safe —
she reached for knowledge in the midst of innocence.
the lilies that breathed their heavy white scent
into eden's air were symbols, so were the angels
that flickered long tongues of fire at garden gates,
and the snake, coiled, glistening with the wet
that grew in eve's belly, the snake
another metaphor that slithered from the mouths
of sunday morning sermons,
daily vacational bible school stories.

i was no eve.
in the midst of knowledge, i reached for innocence.
my life held no symbolic value.
snakes lived in the back yard garden, father's
penis between my legs. the lowest common denominator
that connected the minutes of my days was one
i could not live with, it was too much to live with;
if i had had to keep that fact in my face like my eyes,
my mouth, my childhood would have remained foetal
in bedroom corners sucking its cockthumb, screaming
at dust balls. i wanted more than that,
i wanted to laugh like other girls, play hopscotch,
musical chairs, pin the tail on the donkey,
i wanted to learn 1+1, i wanted to create
für elise and later *liebestraum* on the keyboard,
i wanted to believe in boys. to do this
i could not know, and not to know one's self
means the self must come apart, into selves;
like a deck of cards, selves in suites
played to match the rules of the game going on
around them. in school, there were the selves
that scored As and Bs, in maintenance closets,

the selves scored on by boys in my class.
at home, there were selves to practice the piano,
go to church, love mommy and daddy, make
the morning bed and finally, there were selves
to spread wide as the foundation of despair and amnesia
built to hold everyone together for father
was coming in through the doorway of greatest pain
and the selves that waited for him could not be known
by those who sang *o canada* at the beginning
of a schoolday. there, knowledge of a different sort
was to be taken in; it was played in suites of
diamonds and hearts, three-ring binder paper,
plaid pencil cases, title pages;
family violence did not exist and neither did
the selves who lived it. the world around me
refused me safety, refused me innocence;

i created my own innocence. i came apart.
i delegated knowledge to the selves who carried
the queen of spades in their thighs, delegated
forgetting to selves who had to shut spades and clubs
out of childhood ABCs, hide 'n' seek,
little house on the prairie, jesus.
they could not coexist. when it comes with terror,
knowledge does this to you. you do not argue,
you touch the mark of living death
to the foreheads of the selves who live with it,
then turn your back on them, build the safety wall
to keep them out and smile at the good morning
faces on a world that is reaching out for you.

black bethlehem star

christmas turned us all inside out.
pictures of father, under the wreath.
he was like a black hole, no warmth in the eyes,
the rest of us in orbit around him.

with birth, the explosion into time and distance,
the movement away from parent, light years of travel.
but we held his secrets. he had deposited
imploded constellations in us. his hand never left
us. we wore the same skin, merged to his despair.

in the pictures, the way he watched us.
his eyes like scissors cut us out of every context,
strung his children, hand to hand,
like a paperdoll chain, blank-faced, un-sexed.
on christmas eve, we stood about the piano
and he dragged our voices across the keyboard,
his hands and arms clutching at chords
like a ship's captain at the wheel of a night storm.
in the tall white kitchen, my mother arranged cookies
on melmac plates, smiled at our harmony.

christmas was when god sent his son
into woman, into world, into distance. jesus,
he held god's secrets, god's dark cosmos, as all children do.
it is there in the christmas photos of god's eyes—
knowledge. any parent should surrender life for a child,
but this god sent his son to die, instead.
jesus died for god. jesus carried god's guilt into genesis,
into the world of his flesh. this is what christmas celebrates
and father, sucked-in star that gave out no light,
rocked gently on the piano bench before the baby grand,
pulled us after him into *o little town of bethlehem*
while through the lace curtains, the neighbours' houses
strung with green, red and white, winked on and off,

sometimes there in the night.

about father, we, the paperdolls, were a half-
circle that might connect about him, repetition
on all sides, tightening like a noose. he thought
our silence, paper thin, held the balance of power,
that he, having deposited his rage and terror within us,
was now reduced to reaction

but we were only young stars in orbit,
sending out our small light. we knew where
he began. it was the place our light ended.

after the resurrection

the time we came back from the easter church retreat.
all weekend we had been released, out among the legs
of adults who stood about holding dessert squares
on paper napkins, coffee in styrofoam cups. above us,
they laughed and talked god. their singing followed us
everywhere. down by the beach, faint on the wind,
as we collected gleaming pebbles. solid,
more brightly coloured behind the wall of the next room
as we watched flannelgraph boards, sunday school papers,
practiced sword drills. winding back from their
nature walk, while we threw ourselves into potato sacks,
egg 'n' spoon races, dived into hide 'n' seek.
all weekend we hid among the church congregation,
believed ourselves souls called out from the sepulchre,
stone rolled away from our throats, risen and redeemed.
even late sunday afternoon, swinging our legs
on the squeaking stack-easy wood and metal chairs,
the singing of the adults loud and heavy
coming out of their bodies right next to us.

out of the fading chorus, we drove home. father
discussed the afterlife with the man in the front seat,
mother in another car with this man's wife,
us five children in the back, all under the age of eight.
he warned us to be quiet, but there was god in us still,
echoes of the weekend's singing wafted into our ears,
sent eyes out of car windows into the spring.
our voices darted, wheeled out of us
like sparrows. our bones flickered, note to note.

then father dropped the man, guardian angel,
off at his door — they lived like us. silence
laid itself over us like armageddon coming out of
the man at the steering wheel. we had been noisy,
too alive with sound when he had been full of words

for the man in the front seat now gone. we drove
through flowering streets toward the familiar, tried
to keep hot terror from sluicing out between our legs.

home, we ran, sent to the attic, tripping up three flights,
skin shrinking about us, mother not home yet.
out the gable window, row of chickadees on the hydro wire.
no order to our fear. child closest to father
grabbed first into the body of terror, fist, foot, belt

and the rest of us, sinking into the decay of our flesh,
forced to watch. faces melted out of our eyes.
potholes, huge as night, whirled open in our palms, throat,
gut. we could not hear the sounds we were making.
god was leaving us. the weekend was over. again,
the family began.

let the children go

five pm with the cbc news, the scream
of the oven door opened and closed,
my mother aproned in silence and the scent
of her anger rising up the dark stairs
to where the five of us, noses in books,
floated on our hunger. eddies of chopin
from father's music studio, crept up the stairwell,
lapped at the corners of each room.
we washed our hands in the round basin
under the bathroom mirror that gave us back
head and shoulders but nothing underneath
and descended from the second floor of beds
and books, deeper into the currents of bach,
the smell of food. at the table we waited;
dvorak ended, the swinging door burst
out of the wall and he would be there, father,
the beard, eroded shoulders, the dark eyes
that shot reflected light back at us,
children strung out around the table, suddenly
each an island, full of human need.

always he would clear his throat of some bad taste,
greet our mother ready for his kiss by the stove,
carry the ominous silence toward his chair.
the high white ceiling arched further up and away.
we hunched over empty plates as father prayed,
forgive us. our hunger, larger than faith,
loomed in the stretch of bone, muscle, brain.
slit-eyed under father's words, we watched
steam force its way out from pyrex bowls
of roast beef, carrots, potatoes.
we would come through any fear to get this;
again and again, hunger drove us home.

when father reached for the margarine, alarm
leaped from one of us to the next, a pebble skipping
waves, the closest ducking into the next

and so on, away. my sister, seated beside
father had a line of indigo brown bruises
splashed along her inner arms. easiest to reach,
she would slide onto the bench along the wall,
shroud her fidgets and giggles and stare at food
that sat inches in front of her just on the other side
of his approval, wide as the red sea
and no dry land to get her there.

on the pantry bulletin board, five snapshots
of third world children in torn tee shirts,
eyes hung among thin bones. children of spirit,
father sent them his name on a monthly cheque.
it brought breakfast, lunch, supper, snacks, god.
eating, they believed. it was the same for us
and father knew it. *forgive us,* he prayed
and still the dark cells multiplied within us,
blood rushed to feed them, stomach and bowels
pushed the stuff through. there was nothing
i could do to stop this. black hunger
reached up my throat and took everything in.
at the other end of the table my sister sat,
thin in her purpling flesh,
afraid to pick up her fork.

late evenings, sleep slid into my eyes.
piano lessons still swirled in father's studio
but now i saw the ocean peel back to dry earth
and beyond this the promised land, there for all
who walked in spirit between those walls
of water held up by faith. in silence
i stepped out of pure, moonwhite bones,
handed my skeleton, tinkling like wind chimes,
to father as gift, receipt for his love,
proof of my faith in all that he believed

but life was in me, breathed in and out
of every pore, took back those bones
and would not let me go.

camping

distance unfolds and shakes itself in the map
our mother mutters over in the front seat.
allday we sit on hot vinyl, chew dried apricots
and *triscuits.* concrete section in the american
highway click off one-second intervals.
three hours into the trip, my sister mumbles,
i left my glasses at home. father laughs
like a road sign flashing by too brief to read.
we drive on into my sister's blurred vision,
a radio song let loose on the landscape;
one tin soldier, the sounds of silence.
i watch the tent trailer, wait for the hook-up
to dissolve. under the bleached tarp,
sleeping-bags, clothing, tomatoes and cold cuts,
all we can take with us but it can vanish
sudden as the house on ottawa street when
the van turns the corner and the veranda tears
itself from our gaze like a wild white bird,
but that is the way of it; you hold the moment
like a living thing until larger hands take it from you,
break your hands off at the wrists and take them too.

washington's face pushes up out of mountain rock.
in museums, sepia figures stare back out of civil war,
the depression, norman rockwell turkey dinners.
the green and yellow panic of insects explodes
across the windshield. in evening light
our reflections surface onto the van's window glass,
miles running on beneath our faces a history,
a geography we cannot touch.

at the site, bright-coloured shouts of kids
from other families come to us, greeting cards
sent from far-away. father's fingers dig in

under the lip of the tarp, snap it up and off.
he stalks the land he has paid for, looking
for ground firm enough to carry the weight
of this one-night home. our arms, roots of pain,
children hold the yellow ground lines taut, keep
the shape of the tent alive, waiting for father
to anchor it, our faces gone blank as yesterday
as his fist finds one of us, hammer on a ground peg.
each blow drives us farther under but we keep
that silent line tense and tight between our teeth.
he must inflate, rise, above us the only landmark
familiar and absolute in this wilderness.

the styrofoam cooler lid squeaks, the kerosene stove
is pumped into its blue circle flame, melmac plates
give their dull knock on picnic table wood.
after supper, we squat on cold toilet seats, chant
from toilet paper dispensers, *sanitation
for the nation.* crawling into sleep, we zip it up
around us, lift the long sleeping-bag tongue
and push our goodnight feet against the bum
in the upper cot. we float out from ourselves.
the lake darkens up to our nostrils,
the sun a last bright swallow down the throat
into the dark heartbeat of night crickets
and small-footed dreams come padding up
the rise and fall of deep breathing skin.
hoards of wild and silent teeth surround us.
they gnaw the ground lines through.

baptism

twenty-three of us to be baptized this sunday evening,
each in white floor-length gowns,
lead weights sewn into hems. at the pulpit,
pastor jones bursts out of mouth and hands
like a disaster movie. about him, armageddon
glows in primary colours. backstage,
our baptismal line-up lapses and shivers
along the cold concrete hallway, cold enough
to be the catacombs. girls stand, knees pressed
tight; our thighs work overtime to keep everything
together and in its proper place. the gowns hang
heavy as evening drapes. i think i am a window,
the evil in me will pull the drawstring and
suddenly i will be exposed, the belly roll,
the twelve-year-old breasts someone has plopped
like raw dough onto my chest, some bad joke
my brothers refuse to stop telling.

seventeenth in line, i watch the white backs ahead,
twenty of us under voting age, flow up the stairs,
step one by one into the wound of the organ.
it bleeds as jesus did. saturated with repentance
and four-part harmony, i walk to the baptismal tank
where pastor jones looms out of the organ's groan.
do you believe? he demands, the clutch of water
now about us both. *yes,* i whisper,
lead weights pull my body under,
i am lowered into the water's quiet applause.

it closes overhead like a chest pressed down
across the face. i cannot breathe, know i must
let the water finger me as it wills;
then it will take away my sin the way it took away
the air. i cannot hear the organ, only the heart
steady in my ears and hanging onto this world;

even it begins to doubt. silence slides itself
over me like a pale bedsheet.
death is the moment we search here,
deep in ourselves a shipwrecked treasure.
then pulled back up into life; air and sin
rush into the lungs. i breathe deep.
pastor jones swells in his skin, steps almost direct
into forever. the organ explodes with praise.

wet gown loud about the body
i have renounced and been handed back
like an unforgiven deed, i reconstruct
faith about me like the thin scaffolding
i see hanging onto cathedrals,
shiver off down the hallway past the waiting robes,
their eyes on my sculpted buttocks,
the long wet snake i leave behind.

what i carry away from the platform's edge
just beyond pastor jones's reaching hand
are the underwater lights that shimmer
like the heart's secret place,
the water's stretched-out blue,
eternity lapping at my hemline
like anything of this earth.

trust

sunday mornings my mother heated coffee cakes
with brown sugar topping. we sisters untied rags
from our hair, brushed out snags and tears
while my brothers slid white shirts and ties
over blue and purple bruises, polished
their good shoes brown and black. my favourite
were red leather buckle shoes with flower shapes
cut out across the tops. i wore them until my toes
bled, walked up the broad church stairs,
my frilled dress and hat the front page
of a sunday school paper. at the door, the minister
handed himself out like a street corner pamphlet.
families traded greetings, auctioned off smiles
and gossip. sunday school in the basement was stories
of angel wings wide as a horizon, missionaries
eaten by lions and cannibals, blood-spattered
king james versions planted in jungles
under the screams of strange birds,
the death paws of cats. for the sermon,
we collected in church pew families. my bare legs
made kissing sounds on the bench. we drew
on hymnal pages with the edges of dimes, sang,
this is my father's world. above us,
the ceiling soared heavenward. coming down
the aisle, an usher's face, arm, white shirt front
would be caught out by window glass, suddenly
green, scarlet, purple-blue as hidden skin.

in this world, something had to be true.
we watched for it the way you look for
the missing person in a family photograph.
our eyes were bruises, there in our faces. nobody noticed
us, but we saw the difference in other children,
invisible happiness wove itself through their skin,
they were soaked with it, shouted and laughed

in different colours, so we knew it was out there,
that chance at what they had, if we could figure out
how they'd gotten it, all that love in their blood
while our hearts followed a cycle of sadness,
waxed from full to sickle moons and back again

though we fought it. my first sentence
came with father serving ice cream, my mother
saying, *just give me a little bit,* while i made
my high chair demand, *don't give me a little bit—*
i want too much! they laughed. by the time
i finished high school, my yearbook grad comment read:
the more you give, the more you receive.
i have given myself to the lord; he has given me
more than i have ever dreamed. i had learned
as well as my mother that what i wanted of everything
was less, and god was the place to go for this,
god would take it all, would take me away from myself.
week after week, i dropped a dime and my body
into the offering plate, week after week,
he gave me back beth the spirit, beth the soul.
it was temporary, it lasted only until the next
fist or rape, the next man father offered me to,
my wrists and ankles tied to the piano bench legs
in the soundproofed basement studio; sometimes
he forced my brother mark to warm me up for an audience
that stood, tight-angled with expectation, this violence
bringing their nerve ends, their breathing alive,
while my brother's tears fell, warm rain upon my throat.
beth the spirit could always forgive and forget;
this was just another jungle, beth the body
another blood sacrifice—it was all about blood,
after all, the question was only: *who would give it*
this time? never beth the spirit. she was the word
never made flesh, what she believed could not
be touched or bruised, it was an easier truth,
one that belonged to bedtime prayer, sundays

that were like birthday wishes, except
they came after all the candles had been blown out;
dreams gather strength in the dark, defense against
what lurks in the light, and sundays were like that,
a short escape from truth into god who loved me,
god who forgave me, god who shaped
the hated body into that hilltop cross
and let me die upon it.

the star girl

the other church drove itself in night cars
across country roads to farmhouses, provincial parks.
in these places trees breathed as they did
on ottawa street, but hungrier, with deeper lungs.
through the black of the car window, i would push up
through heavy eyelids to the far-away
and there i would see her, the star girl, somewhere
past orion. veiled in the milky way, she took
star after star into her palm, swallowed it
to clean herself out. watching her, i could
penetrate the distance, kill the seconds between now
and her but as the car turned the family down
a blacker road, trees tore her away; i dropped back
into my groin like a stone.

this road led to the white robes.
they were hooded, carried people with the
human gone out. we all wore them, heavy white,
only skin underneath. the robes believed in god
and jesus and they believed in blood sacrifice.
jesus had always been about blood,
not sunday morning grape juice; in this church
your body was your cross. *now make your body
into a cross,* father said as he taught me about god
and my bed. *now spread your legs. say,
jesus, i love you. jesus forgive me.
now daddy is going to give you his sins.
this is how you die for daddy's sins.* i died,
how many times i died. our shoes piled up
in a farmhouse front hall, we all changed into
naked under white, gathered in rooms where shadows
slipped in and around us, shadows that could touch
and be touched. here infants were baptized in blood,
penetrated with a tiny crucifix base; the base widened
with the years. at three or four, i stood

in full naked squirm before a congregation silent
except for their eyes, while the minister said,
this is the way you can be god's girl,
a good god's girl: sent to another man's lap,
spread-apart legs, crucifix sliding in and out.
sometimes long curved knives cut vertical
across a lower throat, then horizontal, chin to groin;
god imprinted on the edge of every extreme,
my fingertips slashed and bleeding with the jesus sign,
the scars there still. there were altars,
child after child laid out and when we grew breasts,
produced our own blood, there were the crosses,
erected high in that flickering candledark.

arms tied along the horizontal bar, i was salvation,
the bride of christ in white veil and wedding dress,
blood a black-red stain thrown across the front
and then the knife cut away the white and i became
the whore of babylon, slave of the flesh, abomination
that must be nailed to the tree. *this whore must die,*
a white robe intoned. *she must carry your sin*
to the grave. which man among you has sin to nail
to this cross? which man among you is without sin?
no man was ever without sin, since the beginning
god had seen to that, each man mounted
and saved himself as the congregation praised god
for my sacrifice: *blest be the tie that binds.*
the old rugged cross.

in this church i learned god wanted
to see the world coming down my throat,
shoved between my legs; he would use animal,
vegetable or mineral to do it; he would do it to me
because i was. he had created me virgin
to be raped anywhere, anyhow, anytime; for anyman
i became the doorway unto himself.
it is always the body that is the door to the spirit,

spirit the self forced out of the body, pain
the way to do it, pain coming to the body
everywhere just like the possibilities of love and
everywhere is everypore, everynerve end laid bare.

submission corrupts.
absolute submission corrupts absolutely.
there was a way to create spirits god knew nothing about.
he created my body, i created my salvation;
each time god broke me open, the body lived
and someone died. i sent each demon out
into what i thought freedom, what was unutterable
loneliness. they blew through night trees, writhed
in the earth i walked across, they were the shadows
that twisted, darted about church candle flames.
one rose as far into the night as hope can travel
to where stars hung like ripe apples within reach.
it was not quite far enough. as sin gang-raped
the body below, the star girl swallowed infinity,
sky and stars travelled in a straight line
down throat to groin, spread vertical across chest.
as dawn rose in the beaks of early birds,
she hung, that last groan in the dark,
bodycross a white scar, fading into the morning light.

memory code

the very little girl lies on her back,
her naked self still with her,
she still likes skin. then they are here
again, the white robes, hooded faces,
swish of evening drapes the sound of their approach.
hello, beth. her mother's voice is in one of them,
carefully adjusted like a radio volume knob.
they come around her sometimes like this,
white shadows in the dark and it starts.
first one puts fingertips somewhere on her,
begins the slow light circles, the whisper,
beth, beth, beth, then another, another, always
the circles slow, drifting like leaves in a breeze,
beth, beth, beth, all these leaves caught in her skin.
they lift and travel round and round,
sometimes across the surface of her chest,
soft through the inner elbow,
trickle along the ankle, all the white robes
now tracing glad leaves into her skin:
beth, beth, beth.

they could be butterflies, they could be white birds
rising from somewhere deep to meet this touch,
at the edge of herself, she is a great flock
floating across the sun. the finger that touches
and touches her mouth slides in, moves gently out
and in: *beth, beth.* her head spins round and
round like the rest of her, so many separate
circles going round: *beth, beth.* wind coming up,
the pile of leaves lifting, circles growing bigger,
whispers so fast and a finger pushing in below.
she is coming apart, she wants to come apart, away
from the name: *beth.* that name holds her together,
holds her inside the too much, it is too much,
she cannot keep the circles in place, they

push up and out, she finds the tightest darkest circle,
lets the others spin off each alone into itself,
and whirls herself away

into nothing. into quiet. into the still. here
she can hover above that body that looks
still in one piece, the fingers that pull it
every which way while the robes
bend into their whisper: *beth, beth, beth.*
she wonders where the other circles went, if they
still spin in the skin of the girl who lies
below her within the name, the too much,
or if they have spun off, too, into different corners
and angles of this room. they could be anywhere,
she hopes they have gone far away, so far
they take the too much with them out of that skin,
mouth, the down below. when the white robes
swish slow away, she drifts down again
toward the body, its trembling sob
in the alone dark; there is less of it now,
only the memory of the too much
and the memory circles within the places they touched,
skin, mouth, the down below. *beth, beth:*
the very little girl has learned she can
go far away from this, the too much,
there will be so very much more of the too much;
she will let the body take the many soft circles,
the name, the fingerpushingpain, it will have nothing
to do with her, not even the memory of it,
she will spin away into a white bird flying
as far as the white robes send her,
and when she comes home to roost, it will be
to a body somewhere in slumber,
always in slumber, storybooks, dreams.

happysad

i wanted to live in the eaton's christmas
catalogue, its gloss, burgundies and greens,
everyone in housecoats, smiling at wrapped gifts.
they had that bright, slide-off happiness,
the coloured decorator icing we poured onto cookie
shapes—stars, angels, bells, reindeer, santas.
we licked the muddled rainbows that dried
around their edges on plates. our home was a series
of browns, the rooms held some of the usual:
pillow forts in the attic, monopoly in the dining-room,
michael aaron piano books on the old upright
in the underground studio where we practised
scales and triads. summer evenings rolled down
among the houses on our street like kittens at slow play
as we scattered into hid 'n' seek, the neighbourhood
full of emptiness like magazine pictures.
we had a front porch of geraniums and garden chairs,
in winter the front walk was shoveled for easy access,
father kept our school pictures, our tentative smiles,
on his front-of-the-house studio mantel.
in the kitchen, our mother taped school shadows
we brought home, profiles cut out of black
construction paper, glued onto green or red backgrounds,
to the fridge. in this house where the garbage
was always taken out on time, two brothers
shared a goodnight ritual:

> *Q: wanna hear a killer of a joke?*
> *A: it's about a murder.*

they laughed, their guffaws came out of them
bruised a murky yellow, truth wove itself
through fiction like my grandmother braided rags
into throw rugs for bedroom floors.
sometimes, we burrowed under those attic pillows,

fought each other for cover as father's rage
mounted the stairs outside the door.
we listened to opera pour out of the cbc
while my brother vince, seven years old, sat
with his day old socks stuffing his mouth wide,
sat so long, drool soaked his shirt and shorts
and he thought he'd wet himself, all this
because he'd giggled at a soprano. the rest of us
hoped against the hope of being heard, being
noticed, caught on a white sheet spread
on the floor. from a blurred tripod, light so bright
i tried to blink it away, the penis pushing at my
soft mouth, father's voice saying, *now smile*
for the camera, and my mother beside him,
honey, you've got to smile for the camera,
then father again, *he's going to put it in*
like daddy does. put your hands on it and push
it in. smile for the camera. now he wants
to put it in your bum like daddy does. turn
over. upside down like a stomach sliding toward fear,
the world tilted as father held my legs apart
for the white husky to lick, laughed,
frosty's just being friendly!, forced me
into position for a dog mount, shut me into
a closet with nothing between me and that growl
except the dark until i learned to stand, bent,
hands on the floor whenever the dog wanted:
fear of the act was a dog's hair worse
than the act itself and father could always
put that on show, sell a dogfucker's terror
for what it was worth

just like spelling tests taped to the fridge,
front porch geraniums but not the flowers
that grew on the second floor wallpaper.
it was a raised brown pattern. i would stand alone
in this hall, listen to father's preludes and fugues,

smell my mother's ham and apple betty, and i would stretch
my five-year-old hands as high as they could reach,
scratch at those wallpaper flowers, petals
packed to chalk dust under my fingernails,
while the small girl's voice that singsonged only
in my head, chanted, *happysad, happysad.*
all i knew then was *happy is the smile,*
sad the blood that runs through it;
to keep alive you never let blood surface,
people scream at it, they scream your screams
though they don't know it, would not believe it
if they heard them come from your mouth.
life is *sell the happy, bank the sad;*
let father arrange the merchandise.
when i was six and he was five,
i asked my brother mark,
d'you think we'll ever be happy?
he said, *no.*

the only thing father could not sell
was mark's suicide note.
father found it first, showed it only to me.
the last line read: *i wouldn't have lasted this long*
if it hadn't been for vince. father never showed it
to vince, never showed the true picture to anyone,
tried to paint over beige the second floor hall
scratch marks, but little ones haunt it still;
they are tearing the walls down.

separate rooms

what we shared, we never discussed.
in separate lives, my sister pam and i
entered our separate bedrooms the same way.
standing in the hall, the light walked fingers
up and down our backs. ahead, the dark room crouched
around the knife edge of colour the doorway sliced
across the foot of the bed. in this place, something
waited. waits. pretend it is a game, part
of a *nancy drew* plot. measure shadows, angles of sound.
then, slide the hand over the ribbed doorframe
onto the soft pores of hockey wallpaper painted over green
except for the goalie that lurks behind the radiator base.
the light switch, a black plastic knob father installed
upside-down, clicks quieter coming on down.
light: bed, dresser, desk leap like panic and freeze.
everything in this house is under siege,
to be seen is to come under attack. heartbeats
splatter like the beginning of rain across bedspread,
bookshelf, the overhead lamp. wait for the room
to calm itself, lose its neon edge. still, do not go in—
there is the crack between door and doorframe to check
for the hiding man. when he cannot be seen,
slam the door hard against the wall
in case he has learned invisible skin.
above the doorstop shock, listen for his gut grunt
of surprise, then pull the door out so fast dust lifts
in the silence, floats like that grin on father's face,
the one that dangles some secret he never shares.
now slam an arm through closet clothes, the screech
of sliding hangers, turn to face the bed, the dark sneer
underneath and jump into the unknown from as far away
as your particular wings of fear will carry you
up over the abyss that is happening now on the floor
under the bed everything falling away turning
into some other *placetimebodyworld* THEN

and land back in the present tense, the bed's soft complaint,
safe, the moment forgotten in the blink of an eye,
only that blink of an eye taken with every
entry into this room

pam had no doorstop. over the years,
her doorknob left the wall concave. she could
bend into the imagined, look under her bedspread fringe,
but at night she dreamt of the bathroom,
her legs sliding from body-warm flannel sheets,
feet cringing, spreading for a better grip
on an arctic floor. water in the ears, sleep shifted,
tilted her brain like a yawn. she sat on the bed's edge,
a tongue in the black mouth of the room,
nightgown a pale whimper of warning as she stood
and one foot began to rise. then the man's hands shot out
from under the bed, clamped around both ankles
and shackled, pam was falling, pitching into a dark
solid as the floor slammed up against her face.

bedroom window

july evening maples rustle black, landscape
a browngrey sky, watercolour strokes from a weak brush.
from exhibition park, the crack of bat against ball
travels through underwater air toward the girl's ear.
she cradles it like an aggie, rolls it back and forth.
cheers follow, rise and fall like seaweed, sluggish.

head on one arm, the girl floats,
face to the *living* window. houses on this street
squat in shadows that could go anywhere.
three doors up, a streetlight coming on
sketches a porch, shutters in dull yellow.
the girl watches the city scatter light,
confetti across the evening,
into the whispering heave of trees.

she could not say she is trapped in this house,
trapped in her own flesh. she does not know
this room is a genie's bottle, her body is a genie's bottle.
she does not know she wants out.
the place beyond her window moves within itself,
alien and other as it has always been,
traced out like a cosmic fingerpainting
that does not touch her. she is the single
still place. cork pushed down the throat,
anchored in a body that went down a long time ago,
she stares upward to where swimmer legs
kick pale flashes of flesh light, fading shouts
and laughter sent down to her like a depth sounding.
she cannot remember air. she cannot remember
sun. there is only the surface far above,
stained glass window of water and light,
the eyes of the drowned upon it.

secret friends

the girl in the maple tree.
as each night circled, coming down on slow wing,
she settled in her peter pan outfit
on a branch close to my window.
slim boy body perfectly balanced, she kept
her face turned always away to the east,
ready to collect the earliest light for me
on her skin. summer or winter,
she sang all the sentimental favourites—
alfie, send in the clowns, the summer knows,
somewhere – sang them louder when i needed them most,
hummed low in her throat a slow river
when i was safe, just to keep me there.

the silent one gripped the peak
of the veranda roof between her thighs.
cold fury streamlined her like a ship's figurehead,
hair swept back from a forehead
broad and pure as a small sky.
she knew the direction this house plunged toward.
rising and falling on the storm
built into its foundation, walls,
the slow seethe between each brick,
she rode it all out. her rage fixed ahead
like a compass, she stared north to where it was
all horizon, thin line between here and forever.
if we could reach that place, she knew it would be
over, now would be gone, the house settle,
rooms sleep.

another flew window to window, little girl
with long dark hair and a pale nightdress,
palms pressed into startled stars against black glass
and wailing like catherine's ghost to be let in.
there were others, one who drifted

her small naked body into shapes of snow
on windowsills, content just to be close,
one who crept along eaves troughs,
rolling messages to me like chestnuts.
in my bedroom closet lived one who had crawled
up out of myth; a single eye, huge, reptilian,
she opened only to record, document, witness.
she saw more than the eye of god and all his saints
and when she closed she took all knowledge
like the bite of an apple into herself,
spread it through the dna of each cell—
earth, water, fire, air.

their secret voices followed me everywhere,
fingered my body like a gambler's dice. they could
lift me out of any place, slip me out of my skin
like a glove coming off a hand. looking behind me,
i would see a girl who sat on the basement piano bench
while i floated off to a high-shadowed corner,
watched her hands run scales up and down
the black and white keys. one i never saw,
though i know where she lived. sometimes,
my body rolled onto its back, the lower half
faded to nothing, the arms pinned themselves
to the giant carnation on the bedspread
and i could not move. then my eyes
would take the only way out; they rose
like a single angel leaving earth
toward the overhead light, and i went with them
into the thick frosted lamp, its writhing lilies.
then this girl, the secret girl i've never seen,
would come near. she lived in the bed
and she lay there for me. what rammed itself
into those years she took away from me,
she took it all away from me.

now i must go back,

trade places with her and find it.

i searched for my secret friends behind doors,
under beds, in the clothes that hung silent
and ready in closets, but they hid from me.
though they were children, they never played.
when there was work to do, when there was need,
with their small girl faces, thin bodies of love,
they were near to me, they always came to me.
i could not have known what they knew,
seen what they saw, heard what they heard,
and survived. they knew this, they offered themselves
in my place, they took my body and gave me the ones
in the maple tree, the veranda, the overhead light.
one by one, they took what i could not,
they were the best parts of me,
they became the shapes of need.

two brothers

two brothers, one year apart, shared bunk beds
in the room with hockey figures on the swirling walls,
then moved up to the attic. mark, the elder,
with the brown eyes and hair of father, walked into
everything one year ahead and vince, blond brown,
a blue-green-hazel stare closer to mother, watched
what went before and survived it.

at my grade five birthday party, vince
put an entire onion into his eight-year-old mouth,
chewed it raw, face torched like a warning,
but he swallowed to prove he could. i remember
we three sisters playing barbies in the tv room. the door
threw itself out of the wall and my brothers ran in,
vince naked and nine years old, mark clothed,
hanging back and giggling as vince leapt and cavorted,
small penis jerking like a mexican jumping bean,
while we three sisters, wound into one shrill
elongated shriek, stood, hands clasped to our bosoms,
one eye closed firm, the other slit open. i remember
vince on the chess team, the rugger team, playing
the trombone; he carried the swagger of the macho
high school elite. the world was there to take him on;
even in his sleep he was ready, no longer
the five-year-old bedwetter. father broke chairs
and tennis racquets across him, would tear
up three flights of stairs in crazed pursuit
of that tough young body, sun still burning in its bones,
life ahead of it, choices and no children yet to drag
him down, only a father and he would do it—he would
take that boy between his hands and teach him
the shape of fear.

and he did. father was entirely successful.
fear prowled the boundaries of vince's skin,

shone on his nakedness, fine gold hairs.
what surprised both father and son
was the coldness of it, glinting in the face
of the father's dark rage. *when he beats you,*
vince said, *don't make a sound.*
you girls, you cry, you scream. you give him
what he wants. i take it away. into the eye of the storm,
the small boy sent out that bluegreenhazel stare.
i *don't live here anymore,* it told father.
you can hit this flesh and i will laugh.

but mark stayed within the confines of blood, bone,
heart, moved farther and farther in. after, we found porn
magazines between his mattresses. the goodbye picture
he took in the drugstore photo machine two weeks before
his death shows pupils had swallowed irises; already
darkness had come up from inside to shut out the light.
sometimes father, hands around mark's head, would slam it
against the attic, the kitchen, the living-room floor,
like a jar of peaches whose lid won't open,
vince fluttering behind them, blond candlelight, next
in line, but father did that to all of us, broke the seals on
all of us, something to clean up off the floor.
and mark was the class clown, the one who put on
nylons for a high school assembly, imitated joe namath
in *l'eggs.* lips against the brass tuba mouth,
he played the school band, hallways, football game crowd,
oom-pah-pahed his way home up the ottawa street hill.

the last summer, he was fifteen, we worked together,
pulled weeds at the university agricultural plots,
biked back and forth. i remember him asleep in the shade
against a tree, knees up, the wide legs of his cut-offs
slid to one side so his scrotum surfaced, pale
with small bumps like a chicken drumstick
and me staring, not knowing what it was,
but i do not remember a single conversation

before or after he stole the van, did the b&es,
began the weekly probation officer visits, awols,
came back from florida, hands behind himself in cuffs,
twisted into the shape of the six o'clock news.

what i remember most is this:
the slow tread of his feet on the stairs, passing by
the second floor on his way to the attic, the way
those sounds carried loneliness, trailed after him
up the stairwell, long and weighted, an invisible cape.
and i see him opening and closing the fridge,
eating like the rest of us.

clues

in the funeral home viewing room, my sister pam
waited until she was alone, leaned into the coffin,
shifted the collar on her fifteen year old brother's sunday suit
and memorized the purpleblack circle around his throat.
for four years after, she told everyone mark died
in a car crash. the day before, she had walked
into a thursday afternoon house to find silence,
no notes from father's studio crawling
up and down walls like his disembodied hands.
standing at the mantel, father turned, said,
maybe you should go do your paper route now.
she travelled door to door, tossing headlines
onto everyone else's front step, that shoulderbag
of far-away faces and events that had nothing to do
with her thirteen-year-old heart, her return
through april snow to a kitchen where father
and mother assembled leftover children, said only,
your brother is in heaven, and no one cried.

always the youngest, she followed, fifth in line,
the trail of footprints we left across town
to the christian school, junior high, high school,
always in pigtails, shrieks and squawks, giggles.
her nickname was *skweech,* her high chair vibrated
under her pounding spoon, she travelled at a volume
and speed double her years to keep up.
for her, like the rest of us, there was no respite.
on early feet, so young the front yard was a new world,
she remembers father upended a bucket of water on her
with a force that knocked her down, self
suddenly a lung driving up for air. or, as she
searched for hidden cookies on basement shelves,
his approach folded her body into a thin line of terror,
she ran to hide behind a barrel but he saw her,
without a word collected boots and shoes drying

on the nearby furnace, threw them one by one
at her six years, cowered into the smallest
circle of nothing her body could make,
threw them hard, steady as a heartbeat,
aimed for whatever fear her thin arms could not cover.
finished, he left, the explanation as silent
as the bruises that would surface into the throb
on her arms and legs: *he is here, terror happens.*
he chooses when, where, how and you
must be the why of it—he does it to you.

i was the eldest, took her into closets,
pulled down her pants so i could spank that bum,
bare buttock giving against my palm, sensual, something
i wanted to push pain into, push hard into
her soft whimper, bent over, crouched in the dark,
then the door pulled suddenly into light, father's face,
his knowing. by grade three, my sister had lost
her gag reflex, could pick at tonsil pus pockets
without muscle interference, again the reason:
this is you, the way you are, the way you have always been.
the time a horse kicked pam's forehead,
she woke the next morning in the lower bunkbed
to find the sister she shared the room with
leaning down from the upper bunk, her fingers
picking at pam's newly sewn stitches;
how often we fingered what held each other together —
the itch to yank the hanging thread, watch
face and hope come apart. what lay underneath?
it was the same place in each of us, we tiptoed
around its outer edges, tried to push each other in,
sometimes stepped on fingertips that clutched
the cliff edge, other times stood over that death drop
and lent out our wings. now we remember
each other's pain as if we had always felt it together,
always breathed one another's air — the time
mark strung a bubblegum necklace for mother's day

and father ranted it was not enough —
nothing was ever enough, being a child was never
enough, we were all children together,
left trails in the dark, clues for one another that said:
i was here before you. i am here with you yet.

in the hidden cookie jar, pam knew mark had been there
when the cookies were reshuffled in a pattern
she hadn't left; in memory his fingerprints
glow with a warmth she can reach in and touch,
but no one followed behind her.
one summer in montreal's st. joseph's cathedral,
the church that kept st. joseph's heart in a jar
in front of a donation box until it was kidnapped,
the ransom never paid, in among walls
crowded with the crutches of those
who had believed and walked again,
she stood before hundreds of flickering candles,
another donation box to remember the dead.
no one had yet died. she closed her eyes,
wished for something she cannot now bring back
to herself, and blew every candle out.

altar

there was a place my mother went to
as she carried frozen roasts up from the basement freezer,
stared out from the van window at trees crocheted
against grey sky, disappeared into the locked room
to sew clothes for every one of our dolls that christmas.
three times a day, she stepped out of our sound
and movement, went down on her knees to check
the pilot light in the gut of the kitchen stove.
when i was little, she told us, *there was a fire*
in our farmhouse stove. my mother said she found me
dragging my baby brother through thick smoke
and headed for the open door.

sundays, i watched her. hymnal in hand, face somewhere else
like a scene in a painting you cannot step into,
she stood in the family line and pulsed deep in her throat,
praise pouring in through the stained glass windows.
mornings, father's piano lessons already seeping
through the front studio wall,
i'd see her seated on our dining-room couch,
its weave of brown, small specks of red and amber,
her hair dyed a startling solid black-brown
against the pale skin that touched feathery,
soft between its lines and folds. she wore housecoats
we'd grown out of, the pink and purple striped velour,
the aqua blue terry, buttonholes stretched,
zipper pulling away from its seams,
and spilling off her lap the large, leather-bound
bible, its rustling onion skin pages edged in gold,
verses she'd underlined in blue, red, green ink.
she'd taken this bible to university, germany, canada
and on into the birth of each child, had read her life
in it for decades, held her own history between her hands.
when she fingered the worn leather, her skin began
to breathe. inside she would float in story and faith

while i saw the body shaped into questions
bent around those truths, the weight of the word
comfortably heavy on her groin.

my mother was with us on the pantry bulletin board
in the long careful lists of food stocked
in the three freezers, fruit dusky and glowing
among shelves of jars in the furnace room.
she rolled, smooth and slippery between our palms
in the fake pearl necklaces, glimmered
in the clip-on earrings that pushed
small wedges of pain into our lobes.
sometimes, pounding dough, her voice would spiral
into the excitement of flannery o'connor, c.s. lewis,
small town montana's version of the american dream,
and moments of hope and wonder rose out of her
heady as the scent of baking bread. she had a world
somewhere; it had bright, wild flowers, trees
whose leaves murmured of the knowledge of good.
where my mother went, there was no evil

and when father kicked and punched my brothers
and i screamed above their groans, *he's killing them!*
he's killing them! my mother ran from the room,
hands spread wide against the pain swarming her ears.
when i came home from my twentieth century
history class with questions about vietnam,
she retreated into a three day silence.
returning one night from teaching piano lessons
at a downtown music store, i opened the side door,
stepped into the back hallway. my brother had run away
again, my mother had gone with him, following
his absence like the ten commandments,
and as i pulled off my boots, the door at the top
of the stairs was ripped open like a scab,
kitchen light poured out around my mother
peeled of all her skin, bleeding panic, hunched

into her fear. for a moment, she was there, she saw me,
took note i was not the lost one she closed the door
and went away again.

my mother took my brother's suicide into the bedroom
she shared with father, pulled down the window-shade
gone gold and brown with age, torn and mended with tape,
shut those eyelids against a sky vehement with sun.
i lived in the next room. in that dark place,
i would hear her weep, her body clawed with the grief
i could not reach in myself. sometimes i went into
that grey-brown place, went into her sorrow, tried
to touch and comfort her small round body, the dyed head
that reached my shoulders, the soft scent of her bosom
curved in below mine, but she ran from me.
i was not the face she wanted coming in the side door.
on the coroner's report, she told me, *he strangled*
in three minutes. better that than a neck
immediately broken. he had time to reconsider,
offer up his life to the lord.

then in me rose the scream of the body that could feel
rope tighten around eyes, ears, tongue, nose, skin,
lungs that breathed the present tense.
i did not let it through my lips
but when my mother came out of that room,
closed the door on it and went on to lead bereavement
groups, counsel others in their grief, i let her go.
if this was her last, her most complete journey away
from her flesh and blood, her children among the living,
around me i had the memory of that christmas long ago,
climbing down out of windows of bedroom stars
into a dining-room ringed with dolls sewn into frills
and sequins winking blue, red, green in tree lights.
i had her voice, fervent with a faith in symbols
of truth and equality, and i had my body,
fed with years of beef and potatoes, yams and apple pie.

she had given me what she could. it was enough
to lift and carry me beyond what contained her.

a weekend i came home from adult life, my parents travelled
to buffalo. face in the front doorway strained between
my coming and her going, my mother made me promise
to check the pilot light, ensure it did not go out.
mornings and evenings, i knelt before the stove,
opened the door below the oven, placed my cheek
on the cool varnished floorboards and looked up
into the darkness, searching for the small blue fire,
its whisper fragile and pure, glowing solitary
in the black. pressed down against the floor,
staring up into this secret flame, i knew
i had found the place my mother had always gone to,
closed in behind the stove door while we,
amid the chaos, the exploding newness, the birthright
of our bodies, went on around her. she held herself
apart, a light that burned against the dark;
she hoped for us.

young men

sunday afternoons at rockwood park.
lines of light sketch and scatter
across the lake, cut into the eye
with the weight of a skate blade. heat swims,
curves in the air like a lethargic fish.
toddlers in sun hats and oversized waddles
whack the wet sand with plastic shovels
while into the cool shawl of the evergreens,
families spread worn blankets, open coolers.
father sits in a lawn chair, william f. buckley jr.
in his lap, wrapped to his neck in large towels
against the sun, dropped behind sunglasses into a snooze
while my mother fidgets on a picnic bench,
waiting the minute to pack up.
around me the shrieks of brothers and sisters
tossing a three-coloured beachball, inflated
the way a child's heart recreates itself, given
half the chance. i stand on the edge of puberty,
the buoy line where the rocks begin,
watch the place the gorge juts up. hikers climb a path
worn into the rock and pine needle scent;
their red and yellow tee shirts disappear
with their voices into the trees. at the top of the climb,
well back from the path, the warning sign:

DIVE AT YOUR OWN RISK.

the water level is low. rocks wait.
i see flashes of bare shoulders,
wet heads. calling voices ripple. it is the men
approaching the peak of youth, dizzying height.
they have come to this afternoon
from summer jobs, university classes, wine, drugs,
rock 'n' roll. someone turns up a radio: *sweet
city woman.* on the path,

families glance through the pines, uneasy
at the flickers of flesh their children see so close
to the cliff edge and move on. the young men
thrust themselves out against their skins,
pace the gorge that is a breath drawn in.
something pushes up in them fierce,
defined as a clifftop spruce, something
trapped. one by one it reaches their fingertips,
head gone back, mouth open to swallow the last sun
then bright brain exploding, one is falling, he falls
headfirst through the air with purpose,
brilliant intent.

the water is cut, then silence. on the cliff edge,
eyes shift back and forth across the green-black depths.
this is where they go into themselves, sudden,
violent, dive the shallow dark, all hope gone skin.
then the water breaks, the young man rises,
rises through the surface, arms outstretched,
fists clenched about invisible wings.
light cascades off head and shoulders, body raw
and bleeding, fear scraped off and left, curled
into the lick of water around the rocks below.
above him, cheers erupt. he wades toward shore,
while another, dark outline against the blue hot sky,
prepares, mortal, this fall toward grace.

sisters

when i was in grade eight, zambian soldiers
guarding the border along the victoria falls
shot my best friend's sister. our neighbour,
i had seen her in flannel shirts and cut-offs,
flipping pancakes to gordon lightfoot,
backing a station wagon down their hillside drive
slow so the muffler didn't scrape.
that day in '73, she was twenty years old,
balanced with a girlfriend on wet rocks,
the planet packed into knapsacks on their backs
and watching the weight of the outer atmosphere,
a white roar coming down upon them. shots
were fired from the river's other side,
aimed at bright tee shirts that danced
like sun spots, a trick of the light
along the opposite shore.

i remember my friend called over the PA,
how she faded into the hot may day.
zambian soldiers were claiming tourists had swarmed
the zambeze river, swimming to attack the power plant
through an undertow the radio said mark spitz
could not have survived. what i knew was this
was a world in which my british columbia cousin
had a crush on the osmonds. my mother floated
around our kitchen with vicki gabereau, barbara frum,
cbc radio hosts. something kept each day in place
the way i held up knee socks by folding down
the tops around the thin hot burn of elastic bands.
at breakfast, i sat among siblings and read
jam tin labels as if they held the key
to the meaning of life, my lips swollen red raw
with secrets boys took from me among the trees
behind my junior high. each time it was over
i buried the memory like a dead sister —

deep within me so many sisters and no one to mourn,
no flowers placed on these unmarked graves.
blurred by newsprint, my friend's sister's
face made the front page. that afternoon
or the next, i stood in our back yard.
it was raining, tears washed away my face,
i did not know why i was crying, if my grief
was real or if i needed it as evidence
i remained among the living, could still feel
this pain. father's i knew so well.
every time he walked into a room, there was
the little boy in him expecting to get hurt
again, his smile a paper cut before the pain.
solitude rubbed against him, removed layer
after layer of skin until only the bloody surface
remained. everywhere he left small smears
of loneliness — on walls, piano keys,
other people's shirts. i knew this,
i was covered in his blood but the hands
that grew on the ends of his arms, those hands
that took the pure white sound of chopin's lilies,
debussy's falling rain, they also carried guns.
he was the sniper on the opposite bank, waiting
his moment of flesh. three doors down our street,
an explorer of the african continent had come back,
coffin in an airplane cargo hold. i bowed
my head at breakfast table devotions, prayed,
i swim that river. forgive me,
i breathe the devil like oxygen into my blood,
and arrogance, forgive me, it is my weapon,
the life wish i clamp tight and thin as air
like a tongue between my teeth.

war

pressed into the gym, all of us together
one small country, the folding wall split us down the middle,
grade sevens on one side, grade eights on the other.
between us the air beat with invisible hearts, our eyes
fixed on the monitor where hockey figures swirled
faster than thought. overtime in the *canada-russia series*
and the cold war was tied, picking up momentum,
teams skated back and forth like the breath
that swelled and died in each of us.
it was the seventies; the state had no place
in the beds of the nation, not even rosemary's baby's.
trudeau gave us the finger and the buttonhole rose,
atwood surfaced in the wilderness, morgentaler
in the womb. in our house, william f. buckley jr. sneered
on coffee tables, billy graham glowed on tv crusades.
it was all war, the state massing on the borders
of every nuclear family, lining us up for
social insurance numbers, computerized food products.
terrorists made the daily news, we were all booked
on flights predestined for detonation. in junior high,
we wore plaid and velour, that decade
the running shoes and tee shirts were *adidas,* power
was something the other kids wore, loose about the neck
like a scarf, slung over the shoulder, packed
like a knapsack. unnoticed, you could live out
a private pain. noticed, you lost your life.
all of us saw what lay ahead, knew we needed practice,
another's fear as amulet, a knife-sharpening stone,
someone who could bleed and not quite die.
classmates played me like a pair of clackers,
two plastic balls joined by a string, bounced
above and below the hand in regular rhythm
until banned due to the odd explosion
but skin and bone last longer, bruise and bleed,
then clear away the evidence. i never cracked,

retreated in behind the inner lenses of cat eye glasses,
passed two years focused on the quiet reflection
of my own eyes. to look further,
i would have had to see the middle east, vietnam,
patty hearst in our own classroom, myself the target zone,
so i let it all fade, let the external claim itself,
watched that inner eye; it saw a world of peace

and the odd moment a truce snuck up on us,
i could turn my gaze out again, find hundreds
of kids sprawled on a gym floor, *adidas* and polyester
next to each other. that afternoon it didn't matter,
that afternoon nothing mattered, we were all canadians,
the enemy somewhere else and we sat on the edge
of one dream, hearts beating the same rhythm
and then the puck went in, paul henderson's goal
scored. the yell that pulled us up off that gym floor
cut across a continent of time zones,
coast to coast to coast we were fireworks set off,
pinwheels reeled in our brains, rockets exploded
from our mouths, our hands were sparklers
that drifted the final brilliant signs of life
across a black, a summer-gentle sky.

living with truth

grade eight history: *manifest destiny,*
coureurs de bois. the girl was always lost,
waking up in the same bedroom not knowing
where she was, coming from somewhere else,
someone else. father's smile was a spider,
it crawled down off his face. already she
could slip out of her body like a glove
coming off a hand. she was the surface,
visible to parents, teachers, friends,
as the face, the fact of *beth goobie,*
but *beth* was a body lost and found, lost and found
like a winter scarf or a melody she strained
to remember, remember, forget, forget again.

floating in ceiling corners, the girl watched
teachers count mistakes against children,
never the number right, always the number wrong.
only one answer — the one at the surface;
never trust the surface: one is one is one.
math is 3-D like everything else and survival
is the trick of learning to walk on water.
living with something she could not,
the girl changed herself so she did not
have to live with being alive all the time.
born into one name, one body,
but not one life. she was many,
each had a function separate and important
as patches on a life raft,
her body a life raft of patches sewn
with the finest of fairy tale stitching.

this is how survival works.
in the trees behind the school,
one grade eight boy grips the girl's head,
shoves its face into wet autumn earth and leaves

between his knees, while another unzips
her skin down the side along the hip. then
the girl they called in among the trees,
hey beth, come over here,
the one they call *beth* escapes.
another, her name unknown to them, unknown even
to the girl they call *beth,* another, her name
is *jenny—jenny-to-take-the-pain—jenny* rises
to take the first girl's place, rises
into sudden-exposed buttocks, hands
that spread her wide for pain that is always wider.
jenny is a *lazarus:* death and resurrection.
rape her to death, then resurrection back into
body/pain/rape her to death, then resurrection back

into the knowledge you cannot live with you will kill.
jenny was the corpse come back to life
to die again. that was her job. there were many
who had jobs in the girl called *beth.*
there was the one who came to bury *jenny,*
pick the body up off the ground, walk it home
again. and someone to forget, someone who could
walk into homeroom the next day, look those boys
who fucked all *beth's* faces as the same face,
look them in the eye and not blink.
each one's fear had its own smell,
sounded different in the throat.
which was the true one? the girl who did not know
the shape or feel of the penis going off
like a grenade in her own flesh? she sang,
moon river, believed love
was a showboat, daddy would buy her a ticket,
life would perform like the shimmering white
sugar plum fairy dancing for an audience
who watched her from the dark, dreams twisted
and combed out into shoulder-length rag curls.

this girl did not know she herself was the ticket,
did not know the cost of purchase, who had paid.
her job was to seal herself with concrete seams of hope
into a small place within the body she shared
with the true ones. sometimes, a dizzy fatigue
leaned her against bedroom, church, classroom wall
which gave way against her shoulder like inside flesh,
red, squishy, running with the blood
she did not know she had. this was the revenge
of the true ones. they carried pain and rage
for her so she could carry the body through
childhood and adolescence into legal independence
and get everyone, get all of the many,
get them all the hell out.

the girl at the surface used her thumbnail
to wedge red welt crucifixes onto her fingertips.
she did not know why. if asked,
she might have said it was the sign of god,
protection against touching the world,
but it was protection against the true ones.
in the bone, the blood, the tongue,
they held knowledge, they held memory.
it was her own flesh she could not touch.
it was her own life she could not live.
it was the world surrounding her that demanded:
you do not know, you will not know,
make sure you never happened.

the fantasy of no

those sunday afternoons during junior high spent
behind a closed bedroom door not with a bible
but wet thighs and the inside of my head.
outside the window, there would be glad piano rain,
violins in the trees, snow that fell thick and wet
out of the sky's belly. eyes closed, i lay
on the bed and my skin would come to me running
up and down soft inside pullover sleeves and collar,
shift like slow water against the inside of my bra.
breasts rose up and out, sweetness blossomed
at their tips, pulled in that hot dark river down
toward groin. sounds curved, gentle in the throat;
on my palms sweat caught the light
in small stars, but i never touched those places of
pleasure rooted strange, shadowy in me,
for behind my eyelids, along my groin,
the long line of boys waited; touch
would bring them in.

weekdays, these boys, in groups of four or five,
would surface out of the slam of lockers, hallway
shouts and laughter, press in at blackboards,
lunchroom tables, playground asphalt, crowd
and rub against me, their corduroy and denim hips
like a wall of sex moving in, grass fire wind-whipped
in my gut. before they laughed and scattered,
the boys whispered my name, moaned fake ecstasy
because i was god's girl, the one with buck teeth
and braces, cat eye glasses and shirts buttoned
to the collar, hands folded on my desk top while girls
around me in halter tops and hot pants rustled,
shifted in their bodies like wind in fallen leaves

but when i saw these boys, grins twisted
into their faces, soda fizz giggles swirled and rose,
hope in the blood. i would take their sudden
groins and hands, safe in hallway crowds and corners.

it was all i could get and i used it, stroked it,
doubled the memory of their warmth, the quick hard
insistence of shoulder and thigh, metal of the locker
pressed against my back, kept this for sunday afternoons
when nothing was faked and they begged, one after another,
the line of them beyond the closed bedroom door
stretching down the flight of stairs through the lobby
uncomfortable in father's presence, and out
onto the street. now only one boy with me at a time,
beauty slow-opening in my eyes and skin and thighs.
his voice and hands drifted, his mouth, warm-lipped,
silenced itself in against my neck,
tasting my pulse and i would give him that —
the touch and taste of me but no more,
not the breasts, raw with wanting or the thighs
pressed in on themselves to increase the sharp line
of sweet, no more though the body groaned and moved
into shapes that would spread and suck and take him in.

then each boy, anger in his throat, would slide out
threats and the knife, run the edge, sharp
with promise along my neck and still i would refuse
him, one by one, the whole long line of them,
still one word kept them all at bay. i used it,
over and over i said *no,* repeated *no,* multiplied
the meaning of *no* on my tongue, the fantasy
i replayed throughout puberty and adolescence, the story
that lived only within the safety of my own thought,
over and over, it was the power to say *no*
and be heard. sunday afternoons, i was respected,
i respected myself. finally the strong warm bodies
wound about me gave up and faded away. sundays,
i overcame the world, man by man my body
learned it could say *no* and keep something for itself,
for god, for whatever it needed to hold its chin high
above father's sunday evening narrowed gaze
and higher again above the giggling surrender
that would come with next week's hallways,
next week's shame.

diets

i could never understand about the breasts.
through puberty and adolescence i dieted,
tried to rid myself of all that stuff puffing out
on me. it belonged to the *breck* girls —
you could see it under their rounded
pastel sweaters, their sunset smiles.
the moment i knew i had been stalked
was the moment it found me, latched onto me,
never to let go. i was on the toilet,
the underwear my mother had sewn
stretched between my knees and i saw my gut
leaked out red as dreams.

my mother had the pads ready for me.
months ago, she'd bought them on sale,
prepared for this, and when i said, *mom,*
it happened, she knew, she came up smiling,
she showed me the family size box of pads,
huge enough to handle a lifetime;
it dominated the laundry closet, the flowered
and striped bedsheets, the thinning towels.
the radio hummed and crooned, *only women bleed,*
another evangelist predicted the end of the world
that october, at all the downtown cinemas, sharks
attacked bikinis, skyscrapers were going up in flames,
planes crashing into this earth. all i wanted
was to go back to the beginning, stop the food
going into me that pushed me toward the future;
i wanted to walk slow and sure into the bones
to the place where i would find

myself, my small boy's body, the one
who ran and played in the long green meadows,
the wind-rippled daisy-lined roads.
within, no hips, no breasts, no genitals —

my true body held the eyes that had seen
the first universe. now it stared out
at a world collapsing around it.
rising from the bath tub's clawed feet and steam,
my mirror-fogged shape brought confusion.
it was the eating; eating brought the apocalypse
into my own flesh, there was a woman
growing on me that had to be stopped.

she would not allow the small boy,
the heart that lived like a native
in its own flesh. she was bleeding,
she collected her terror in pads pinned
between her legs, she wrapped it in toilet paper
and threw it into the garbage.
the small boy would not have done this
with any of his blood. small cuts he sucked
back into himself. with friends, he pressed arms
and traded blood as promise. in his dreams,
he slew great monsters until their blood
fell like rain, enemies like the woman
who grew about him now, closing him in,
but never did he toss parts of himself away,
stuffing the evidence to the bottom of the pail,
naming it *curse, shame,*
the end of innocence.

high school

for S. and B.

everything is sex.
the school's east windows look out on a world
touching itself alive with morning light.
trees stroked green. rooftops, their shingles
shadowed by dark fingertip lines.
ground level, every link in the chain fence
around the school football field strung tight
with something unreleased. in the distance,
the voice of a teacher drones,
sound on shrinking wings; closer, sensation
drifts like october, amber orange edges
aimless against a blue stretching on into

forever begins with the tip of a finger,
soft opened lip on skin, travels in. i can
go anywhere with the thought of this.
against a desk top, the thousand ridges
in my palms arrange and rearrange;
life forms and reforms in the grain of wood.
across the classroom, a boy.
wet with windowlight, he sprawls out,
tee shirt loose about the neck, collarbone
a momentary flare in a body running
sudden and undirected as windowslipping rain
under cotton shirt, faded denim hip.
all this can come off.
slouched into his lower lip, he is warm,
he is dangerous. it is there in the slow spin
of his pen, along lids that weigh down
his stare out into the sun-heavy leaves.
high-up, the teacher's voice circles, sleepy
bottle blue. everything rounds itself. i come
back through *sine* and *tan, hamlet,* life cycle

of the amoeba, back through moist blurred
lips of flesh to the body travelling in,
into those worlds and places
that take care of me. now i lift
up out of the turtleneck, plaid wool pants,
the *jesus saves* sticker stuck to my blazer,
out through the black censor strips slashed
across groin, breasts, mouth,
leave that face as a decoy
pointed at the chalk's endless monologue
with an erasable wall. that face sucks desire
out of herself like a calvinistic vampire
but i escape her, i escape
the eyes of a world that create her
over and over. i cross this hardwood floor,
bare toes explore small stones and grit,
hair a sly lick against nakedness that slides
over me, defines me like wanted touch;
now breasts, buttocks are present, part
of the soft beige blur i *am*
slipping my hand like a dream into the neck
hole the boy left free for me to enter him,
his skin the edge of a forest parting, molecules
of his lips sliding wet easy, mouths
opening, tongues across my belly, breasts,
inner arms, groin, taste his salt sweat flesh,
the innocent wild cries he sends in through
cells startle, fade, multiply again
at his touch, breath

thoughts of his touch, breath.
it keeps the body sane.

the look at the fridge

it was august. sun in the windowlace patterned
lilies of the valley in free floating dust.
i stood, fingers around the fridge door handle.
the kitchen rose above us, all-around white
but for the charred fireplace under the closed-up
chimney and blue willow plates hung above the stove.
there were people in the rest of the house.
my mother shook sleep out of the sheets.
in the bathroom, father smoothed the day into his face.
my sisters and other brother, dull-eyed, still with
dreams fingering their hair, pulled bright hours
out of their closets. further on in the world
there must have been others, night drifting
from their pores, hands reaching to pick up the dawn.
there was the rumble of traffic along the alley
and coming up dublin street, the knife-sharpener's bell.

my brother mark stood in the kitchen doorway.
the side entrance retreated into shadows
behind him, the end of his fifteenth summer;
he would choose death next spring. he wore the cap
that radiated triangles of red, yellow, green
from its peak and under it he was in a body
coming into manhood, thickened at shoulder and jaw.
the hearing was over, the trial for theft and b&e
would come next month. mark, his dark eyes
the threshold coming into the morning, he
was full of the pain he had caused other people
then made himself carry, double the weight—
this is our social custom. i had taken out
strawberry jam, summer cut, boiled, sugared.
i remember the cold glass there in my palm,
the cap's plastic ridges pressed into my hand
as i turned back into a conversation that held
that day's mundane apocalypse, turned back toward

my brother who understood more than i
the dark bodies of children are paperweights
their parents shake and hold up to catch the pattern
of falling stars, then set down again, empty of all
but the night staring out of my brother's eyes. he knew
he was the anointed one, chosen to show us the way
into ourselves. he had begun now, had taken the first
steps of the journey we laid out for him; on the other side
of the kitchen, he was afraid.

the light about me then, the circuit that flowed
over the surface, knit face and skin and spirit
together like an electric weave, the circuit
shut off for the moment i met my brother's eyes
that morning by the fridge and i dissolved, my face
drifted away like fog and someone came up from inside,
came up from a place where there are no bodies,
no need, no pain. she was all darkness,
she had the move and shift of power, she looked out
of my eyes into that day and gave him the only message
i had to offer, the closest i was to hope,

she looked out at the boy who saw the abyss
widening between his feet and she said,
walk on air. grow wings. learn to throw your pain
out of yourself like a neon frisbee, send it
with a flick of your wrist, hand to hand into the crowd
at a church picnic. watch it travel away into laughter
and grin. you're good at this, better than me.
all your life you've worn your bruised body like a joke,
your loud voice a flag announcing a country of one,
well-patrolled and without need. where have you found
this sudden freedom now to cry out:
the hurt in these bones is a wild wind blowing
me beyond this skin and i can find no way back in.

well find it. turn back on that current of life

that holds each one of us together at the surface;
skin deep the self we work to maintain.
sure the circuit jolts, throws that dark one deep
within you about like a body in the electric chair
and you want to save her, release the scream,
but she can take it and you cannot. this is what
she is for, the function she was created to perform.
look at her now in my eyes. she is strong.
she feeds on pain. if she looks like hate,
she is only what we all need to keep going,
just to keep going on and on. this is eternity.

for that one moment, i was powerful.
i stood on the edge of firmaments.
i could have created galaxies, split the world
into night and day, water and land, flesh and spirit.
years back, when my head had been cut from my heart,
still i had believed. now, with my glance, i divided
my brother from me, his pain from my pain,
his story from my truth. with one glance i did this.
then the power in me, it sucked the white gleaming
off the paint that skinned that whole room,
sucked it into me so that the circuit of light
was there again, it hummed and sang like a halo
weaving the outer me together
and the inner one went down

but first my brother's eyes widened a moment
to take in that little bit of soul i'd sent him
winging across the sunlit room, the knives, forks,
bread, salt 'n' pepper shakers, the hymn of the fridge
and another day beginning. his face staggered,
the boy/man's body sagged under the weight
but he took it all in, pore by pore he absorbed
the only bit of life i could give him.

behind him in the doorway were the shadows

and later, when he had done it,
when finally he took purpose into his hands
and used it to crush his own throat, then,
soft in the east i began to fall,
the last, the most brilliant,
the mourning star.

just after i knew

when i came home and my brother was dead
i began to climb the brown stairs
to his attic room. cold stairwell, it wound
smaller than before, hunched against my weight
and the walls, beige ice, froze my fingertips
to their surface. i left a trail of red-rimmed
fingerprints, splayed hollyberries, thrown ripe
against what was there,

up, up past the landing, the lace-shrouded windows,
the second floor where the rest of us lived, up
to the third, where my brothers slept. cold,
the cold that was always there, heaviest under the roof,
drifted down through the pores. the room
had the half-light of cloud and the maple pressing in
at the gable windows. the weight of the universe
took me then and laid me flat across his bed,
not weeping, just resting, as if there was no more to do,
finally no more to resist. it was the only moment
of calm. peace, the edges of sorrow came out in me then
without effort, like evening stars. for him,
it was over. this was no surprise.

from below, my mother called my name,
as if afraid i would draw too close,
and i lifted back into my body, took back
its weight, pushed up into gravity, the heaviness of air,
and moved on.

my brother's wings

a kind of flight, suspended against mid-afternoon
good friday april blue
between tree branch and the lake ontario shoreline
off the QEW, rope coming down like a keyhole,
his head and neck the key to unlock silence,
the ending of stories, the dark.
still, the light has part of my brother. he cannot escape.
i need it sparkling in the lake's reflection that runs
across his now skyblue stare, stretching out his body
in its series of slow air-bound spirals caused by
the odd-angled neck. was he wearing his many-coloured cap?

this is the way i make myself

walk up to the past, run my eyes like fingers
over the face twisted by three minutes losing air,
eyes swollen with seeing everything, nothing, the hands ...
did they stretch out, that last grasp reaching
like the light of a star headed into forever
or did they curl into fists, each a foetus
sucking on its own flesh

i remember that last year. he'd curve over the piano,
his fingers, feverish, seek out korsakov's
flight of the bumblebee, the only music he played
fluently, the bee trapped in a glass jar, my brother
unable to speak this world's language moaning
in his hands.

cleaning out the locker

in the high school basement hallway, sun poured through
glass in the doors behind me, fluorescent lighting dropped
down walls of numb yellow concrete, simmered along beige
and black-flecked linoleum. in this flood of white, murals
along the upper wall began to pale. my feet long ago
disappeared into this bright. i know one hand
touched my locker, rectangle of space clamped into the row
of grey metal lockers to my left, textbooks and careful notes,
lunch bag, clarinet case and spring jacket in the open door
blurred at the edges, swallowed by the light. to my right,
the music room threw beginner chords at the walls, and above,
two floors of everyone distorted into desks. beyond this
the sky.

my body was there, thick, a wood post keeping me upright,
dense matter that clutched darkness against the advancing
light. the body was there alright, but i sat
along the lower rim of the eyelids, a thin guarded line,
as the vice principal turned a distant corner and came
toward me without sound, his arms outstretched,
careful and helpless, as if holding personal roadkill.
he was the one my brother spent detentions with, one
of the many who had not seen enough, and now his eyes
ran on beyond me through the glass of the push-handle doors,
out into the spring along the ottawa street hill.

i do not remember what he was holding—probably
running shoes, jacket, sawed-off padlock, notes. already
they had taken the textbooks back. i must have placed
my arms in a receiving position. he must have laid
the objects upon them where they rested like the memories
of my brother, light-weight and alien, the life gone out.
for seven months, his locker had been around
the hallway corner where the row containing me
became the wall that held him. i had never seen his locker,

had never seen him standing at it, had never seen him
put on his jacket, take out his books, push the lock
closed, but in that moment i would have known it anywhere,
the missing lock, door slightly ajar, the taken gut.

in that raw light, holding the over-exposed skins, i saw
my brother had neatly slipped out of himself, without
blood, only an absence left in someone else's hands.
it was then, standing in that hallway gutted by light,
the vice principal dark in his suit coming toward me,
the gift held out in his arms became knowledge —
knowledge that death was an option, a choice
always there when other things were not, the shedding
of light, the removal of self from the slammed,
the shoved-closed, the locked-in pain.

now

again, coming out the high school tech wing, the boys
are there, pull up in an old car, block escape
with opened doors and arms. *c'mon, beth, just being*
friendly. give us a little of your time.
a teacher walks by, gives the boys the casual
afterschool grin, with his wave erases the fear
from my face, puts something else there. i am
pulled in, halfway through town the clothes off
in the back seat. *hey, swerve the car —*
it makes her boobs jiggle. ooooh beth, you really
turn me on now.

air is love. when you teach yourself this,
you can breathe it, get it free. even when
father's voice is there, tense and tight
as a wind-up toy ready to be let loose,
telling my brother, *now, mark on top. that's right —*
put your finger in the hole. always use your finger
to find the hole. now, put your penis in there.
that's good. keep it going. you like it like that,
don't you beth? say it, beth. say you like it, beth,
and underneath, softer, on parallel tracks,
mark's voice, his secret within father's secret,
secret with grief, whispering,
i'm sorry, i'm sorry, i'm sorry.

safer to hate and not to grieve, safer
not to know rape waited around school corners, safer
to know i hated my brother but not know why,
not safe to even sense i hated father,
and there had to be someone else to share the load —
too much hate to turn on myself and live,
so i hated mark without context until he hanged himself
and i adored those boys, the menace that muscled
their shoulders, loved father always, wore for him

a daddy's girl dressed in virginwhite;
angel light surrounded me like the afterlife.
i was a concept, father was a concept. i believed
in us both. the only other option was reality.
i buried this deep within the dark
of each cell, each cell a grave, my body
a graveyard, girls and more girls in different positions
of mangled death: boys in a party pack tearing off
lingerie someone had dressed me in,
father and mark working both ends of me
hanging over the edges of the downstairs piano bench,
me at five or six riding mark at four or five
while adults circled, our faces a home
already we'd run away from,
no, this was not

what the whitelight revealed, though they said
it was absolute, its truth would set us free,
free of the dark, flesh, knowledge,
free to live in spirit and illusion so they could fuck
the body without complaint until i took it away
into the adult world, safe, began to follow the path
down my throat into memory, the swallowed screams,
the graves i had to keep digging
to keep up with the selves i had to keep killing,
this trail of tombstones i feel my way along now,
read by fingertip the names
i gave each death: *jenny, pretty belle, ruby, jocelyn,*
holly, naomi, susie, theresa, beth. so many
others. they are rising. i feel them shift in each cell,
whispering their names. in this dark, the dead
girls are taking life back into their lungs, i breathe deep
love into their mouths. trust and time that belongs
now to all of us will bring each one singing, weeping,
full of rage, torment, truth into the present tense
where she will be given childhood for the first time
to cradle as she wills

and mark's heart, clear now with death, cut
like a prism, hangs in the center of our vision.
now nothing comes to us white or absolute; my brother's
i'm sorry, slices everything to human dimensions,
a world coloured with scars of light, bleeding,
understood. *i love you, mark. i love you,*
mark. i can love you now
i know.

permission

to some of the girls it had been given.
to the rest of us it was not.
in the high-windowed classrooms, hallways dimly lit now
by memory, the word-staggered cafeteria, it was not
discussed, subject with an unfamiliar vocabulary.
everything came pre-packaged, like our bodies;
we grew into expectations worn out at elbows
and knees, wore mapped-out hemlines with adolescent
flare. it had nothing to do with outlines of flesh
and blood, though in yearbooks you can pick out
the girls granted permission to live in the bone
and the lip. even at a distance, turning away,
they lean into the camera. the sky wraps itself
around their hair like a shawl. laughter slips
through them, light over icicles. the earth unrolls
at their feet. on the girls football team,
they display a long length of boomerang leg;
whatever they give out will come back to them.

it was simply there in the way the voice
fit into the mouth. we did not think to question.
this democracy had been established long before
any of us became aware it was ours to give or withhold.
the rules did not come from boys, sprawled into grins
and rugby shirts, bodychecking the sun, or teachers
in their endless guardwalk back and forth
along chalkboards so easily erased, nor did it come
from the rest of us, girls who floated
above our bodies, dandelions gone to seed
and waiting for the briefest of winds.

we watched ourselves progress through negative integers,
bunsen burners, the imperfect tense, took off
halter tops, elevator shoes and let evening
slide down over us in necklines so low,

moons came to rest in our skins;
for someone we dressed and undressed,
observed the pale in-between body, glowing
in its unfinished equation. we were
the first draft of the great canadian novel;
in us stories were telling themselves over and over,
the way the wind repeats itself soft among the maples,
never losing interest, any of its pain.

if we could have gone back to the source,
had been able to push past the gloss of magazine and tv,
the boys dangerous in our heart, if we had pressed on
beyond picket fences, supper tables, bedroom mirrors,
back even beyond must-scented diaries
to thoughts never recorded, back into the flesh
that renews itself in each cell every seven years
in much the same patterns

                              there we would have found
what we did not know we carried in those
black and white childhood snapshots. heads at an angle,
we had climbed up out of our bodies on fire escapes.
already we breathed smoke like air.
four year olds with memory burning in our blood,
we had seen enough to know who held the match,
the future flickering out there beyond us.

the girl dreams

the girl dreams of a black fortress so quiet
its silence echoes through the forest around it.
in this place it is always night. she walks
through trees without leaves, bushes that push up,
pain that grows dense out of the ground, toward
the fire the others keep for her. she always finds it
outside the fortress, a ways into the forest and here
are the five witches, dressed in black. she thinks
perhaps they have stepped out of her *macbeth* project
but they have the faces and voices of women she knows,
two neighbour ladies whose laps she always wanted
to climb into, two high school teachers who smile
when she walks in the door and listen to her think,
and margaret atwood. the girl has never read
the edible woman but she knows father hates it;
she is not surprised to find atwood here,
in good company with kind neighbour mothers,
teachers of history and language

and the children. there are so many children.
they cluster around the witches, seem to want to stay
as close to one another as layers of skin.
most of them arrive alone through the dark,
stagger in on feet of fear and nakedness.
it has taken them so long to find this love,
they thought aloneness was the way
of it, did not know there were others to search out.
now they see the witches' fire, small so it keeps
its light quiet. as each child comes, she brings
more butterflies. the forest is covered in them,
dark trees velvet with their sleep.
on each wing is memory, the shape of some pain,
transparent like a moment caught in a film.
this is why it is always night.
day would bring them together awake,

butterflies rising in a great swirl, children
caught in everything again at once, scattering
into such a scream, a scream running straight
for death and so they are careful never to let morning
come into this place. sometimes a butterfly is held up
to the firelight, a memory shivers and is seen,
the child who owns it cries out with the shame of it
but the others are with her now to share its taste —
passed among many, it burns going down
but you live, you live in the eyes of the others
who have seen with you and still want you among them,
want you more now they have seen, have tasted,
have held onto the way you still hoped.

there are many still missing.
this is why these children sit outside the fortress —
more children inside chained to ceilings and doors,
always something shoved between their legs, into
their mouths. waiting by the fire, the girl
who dreams this dream watches the witches
pass out marshmallows and hot chocolate,
watches the children touch finger to finger,
watches atwood begin another patrol
around the fortress wall. she wonders how much time
it will take to read each butterfly wing, she wonders
if she will be able to let the flickering light
of each memory pass back into her own skin,
she wonders if the children someday will join hands,
together approach the fortress wall.
spirits coming back to the body,
without need of door or window,
breath finally taken, breath finally owned,
the children will come home.

love

i nuzzled walls, rubbed against doorframes,
hugged trees black and sobbing in the rain.
this was when skin came alive. i wanted
to feel it, wanted some kind of touch,
the nurturing any small child needs, and walls
were safe, they were easier to pretend with—
if you wanted them to give way, soft
as a bosom or a polyester sweater,
they'd do it, it was your dream-making,
they didn't fight it, let you love them as long
as you had need. they would play mother,
they would fake father; the real goods
were made of brick and plaster.
the inanimate could become animate,
if i wasn't given human love,
i would drag it out of somewhere,
pull it out of a magician's hat,
write it into soft cement,
suck it from a stone. or so i thought,
not knowing how much love i was giving
myself. through walls, i caressed my face.
in doorframes, i hugged thin staggered shoulders.
between flannel sheets, i took a small child's
heart and hoping into my forever arms
and let her go to sleep.

in the still

winter evenings, the back alley shrinks.
above the dull insect eyes of street lamps,
brown-grey clouds hang just out of reach.
not even the whisper of snow falling; the sky rests.
silence lies thick over everything, beige
and sloped along the parked car roof,
the next door wooden fence leaning between centuries,
the startled arms of the pear tree that draws
a dense black out of the earth, up into its trunk.

in this two-toned landscape,
no inner detail worries at the rough raw edge
of a child's brain, her crowded heart.
here, there is no one. nothing moves.
the girl herself is only a charcoal shape standing
by the neighbour's fence, watching the stillness
of the bird bath. she thinks of the seeds
the old woman sprinkles there suspended
inside the cap of snow. the girl's face
is one of these. she feels the shell of it relax,
soften like a shadow into the peace of this
dim place. here, shadows can take any shape —
they are the wings of angels that fly within
solid ground. just under the driveway's surface,
the girl senses the space between molecules
under her feet shift and come together again
each time the spirits pass

and for a moment, the skin of her face is gone,
the promise that lives within is rising,
she flowers into that which believes always in itself,
the way *being* contains all four seasons,
the distance hope can travel from the selves
of the past to the selves of the present,
from the children that survive to the children that laugh

wild dandelion pumpkin wisteria blue.

morning will arrive on busy wings and beaks of light.
the girl knows she owes some of herself
to the day. she will scatter bits of flesh
across the surface, small sacrifices, sun-dazzled prey.
the rest she pushes deep into the recesses
between the molecules of the night-black ground,
for in this utter stillness, she has heard infinity
breathe in, breathe out, breathe
into the rise and fall of her own chest,
the same rhythm deep within the earth;
through rock and dark, angels
always coming, always gone.

eight, before definition

truth felt like canned peaches
on the tongue
the years i was eight,
and the yellow forsythia bush
bloomed in the black and white
year round front porch
family photograph
on the kitchen mantel
next to the faded box
of *trust and obey* verses.

autumn was the sound
of spirits dragging their claws
across the earth,
and the smell of leaves
piled under the maples,
their whirling orange red tears
falling, falling.

i did not know, then,
that one brother
pulled out his heart
and let it go in the wind,
believing it would grow back
in the spring.

the rest of us kept ours
in bibles
like bookmarks,
waiting for meaning
to begin.

Beth Goobie was born in 1959. At birth, she was introduced into a Family-based cult that involved her in child prostitution and pornography and Network ritual abuse. To survive, she told herself stories.

Beth Goobie was born in 1959. She won academic and citizenship awards, achieved her grade 10 piano performance certificate at the age of sixteen, taught fifteen to thirty-three piano students weekly throughout high school, and wrote stories. In 1983, she graduated with concurrent baccalaureates in English literature (she was the recipient of the gold medal) and religious studies from the University of Winnipeg and MBBC respectively. She spent the next five and a half years working with abused children and teens.

In 1987, Beth Goobie began to write stories again. Her twelve published books include *Could I Have My Body Back Now, Please?*, *Mission Impossible, The Only-Good Heart,* and *The Colors of Carol Molev.* In 1993, she began to remember.